INFINITE HOPE

How **Wrongful Conviction,** **Solitary Confinement,** and **12 Years** on **Death Row** **Failed** to **Kill My Soul**

. . . . . .

ANTHONY GRAVES

Beacon Press
Boston

BEACON PRESS
Boston, Massachusetts
www.beacon.org

Beacon Press books
are published under the auspices of
the Unitarian Universalist Association of Congregations.

21 20 19 18   8 7 6 5 4 3 2 1

This book is printed on acid-free paper that meets the uncoated paper
ANSI/NISO specifications for permanence as revised in 1992.

Text design and composition by Kim Arney

This is a work of nonfiction. The events portrayed are presented to
the best of the author's memory and records.

Library of Congress Cataloging-in-Publication Data

Names: Graves, Anthony.
Title: Infinite hope : how wrongful conviction, solitary confinement, and 12 years
    on death row failed to kill my soul / Anthony Graves.
Description: Boston : Beacon Press, 2018.
Identifiers: LCCN 2017035843 (print) | LCCN 2017038075 (ebook) |
    ISBN 9780807062548 (e-book) | ISBN 9780807062524 (hardback)
Subjects: LCSH: Graves, Anthony—Trials, litigation, etc. | Death row
    inmates—Texas—Biography. | Trials (Murder)—Texas. | Judicial
    error—Texas. | BISAC: BIOGRAPHY & AUTOBIOGRAPHY / Personal
    Memoirs. | LAW / Criminal Law / General. | POLITICAL SCIENCE /
    Political Freedom & Security / Civil Rights.
Classification: LCC KF224.G735 (ebook) | LCC KF224.G735 G73 2018 (print) |
    DDC 345.764/02523—dc23
LC record available at https://lccn.loc.gov/2017035843

I dedicate this book to all the men
and women who have experienced
unconscionable injustice in prison.
And for those still going
through it today, hold on.
A change *can* come.

It matters not how strait the gate,
How charged with punishments the scroll,
I am the master of my fate,
I am the captain of my soul.

—WILLIAM ERNEST HENLEY,
"Invictus"

CONTENTS

ACCORDING TO A THEORY put forward by the State of Texas, at around 3 a.m. on August 18, 1992, in the small town of Somerville, a man named Robert Carter approached a trailer home where he believed his four-year-old son, Jason Davis, was staying. Faced with an impending paternity suit and child-support responsibilities, Carter planned to kill the boy. When he arrived, he found six people at the home: Bobbie Davis, Jason's maternal grandmother; her sixteen-year-old daughter, Nicole Davis; and four grandchildren, Brittany Davis, Lea'Erin Davis, Jason Davis, and Jason's half-sister Denitra, all under the age of ten. Carter spoke with the boy's grandmother for a period of time before brutally killing her with a hammer. He went on to fatally maim, shoot, and stab everyone else in the house, his son included. In an effort to cover up the crime, he doused the home with gasoline and lit it ablaze.

Carter became a suspect in the case after attending the victims' funeral four days after the murders; there, he'd been observed with raw burn wounds on his neck, ears, face, and arms. On the afternoon of the funeral, two Texas Rangers picked Carter up at his home and took him to the police station for questioning. After hours of interrogation late into the night, Carter made a statement partially implicating himself and fully pointing the blame at another man. Two warrants were issued. Robert Carter was arrested immediately based on inconsistencies in his story and the physical evidence that tied him to the crimes. The other warrant was for a man with neither a motive nor any supporting physical evidence linking him to the murders, who was arrested based solely on the faulty testimony of a desperate man in police custody.

. . . . .

October 27, 2010. The cell was cold and familiar. I'd been back in Burleson County Jail for more than four years by then, waiting for the resolution of a nightmare I'd thought was over. Bisecting the cell was a long metal table that in another world might have been a picnic table covered with greasy goodies from some well-tended grill. It was hard to imagine this table filled with friends and family, though. I had none in Burleson. I was a "danger" to the hardened inmate population, or so the state said.

Solitary is where they put someone charged with a capital offense, and I was the only capital inmate Burleson had, so it was me alone in solitary, and the double isolation made it worse. The cell was big enough to house four inmates; it was like a big empty warehouse. I felt isolated not only because of my physical surroundings, but because I didn't know anyone in Burleson, and it was obvious that everyone in the jail had been instructed not to talk to me. I was *the death row inmate*, the branding that had determined so much about the quality of my life for years. It was like being a celebrity of the wrong kind, for all the wrong reasons, and all eyes looking at me knew my infamous status. The feeling of being constantly judged was an extra layer of punishment in the midst of an already unthinkable situation: I was on track to be executed by the State of Texas for a crime I knew nothing about and did not commit.

My jail cell was secluded and also cold—so cold that I walked around wrapped in my blanket every day to keep my body temperature up. I talked my thoughts out loud just to hear my own voice. When an officer would come to my cell, I would try to engage him or her in conversation just to interact with another human being. Some would stay and talk for a while, but not often. People never understand how truly important human contact is until it is taken away. I had no human contact. The windows had blinds on them from the outside so that I couldn't look out into the hallway, but someone in the hallway could open the blinds at any time and look in at me. A toilet and shower sat behind a spare metal partition, giving the illusion of privacy. But it was only an illusion. I felt like a creature on display. That is something that is taken for granted on the outside: the expectation of being treated decently.

Of the two sets of steel bunk beds up against the back wall, the bed at the bottom right was the only one covered with a thin plastic mattress. They didn't issue pillows so I ended up balling my clothes and sleeping with them under my head instead. A pay phone hung along the side of the wall beside the seatless toilet bowl. I could use the phone to make collect calls to my family, but the calls were exorbitantly expensive. The color of the cell was light gray, with food stains and small graffiti covering the walls. The whole place smelled mildewy and just plain foul.

A television sat on top of a stand that was mounted on the wall. I could watch the local news and shows that came on the basic channels. Silence had become my worst enemy.

I was only existing in life, waiting for my fate to be determined by other people. There was nothing to do, no obvious way to become engaged in anything. The hours of nothing interrupted by monotonous routine can literally drive a man insane.

I was desperate for human contact. I needed help and to feel the power of being connected to something larger than myself. That was the danger I had sensed from the very beginning. Not the physical kind; this was mental. I was balanced on the razor's edge, and it wouldn't take much to push me into not caring about myself anymore. I knew that if that happened, I would simply be killed by the state, my life eliminated before I had the chance to grow into a person with something to contribute to the world. I hadn't quite discovered that self yet. I didn't want to die before I had the chance.

In order to survive, I distracted myself from my immediate surroundings by withdrawing inward, which is not my natural disposition—but then, these were unusual times. By going inside myself, I escaped the smell, the awful toneless grays encircling me, the chill of the steel, the lack of humanity. I learned to be a community of one. I could only control the tiniest elements of my existence. And so I'd turned to letter writing as a way to lift the suffocating walls of isolation, one bit of communication at a time.

The metal table was bolted to the concrete floor, with steel benches on either side, and seated on one of these benches is where I found myself most of the day. I wrote countless letters at this table. I wrote letters to family, friends, and my attorneys. I wrote to remind people that I needed their help in saving my life. I had developed relationships with people as far away as Paris, Switzerland, Germany, Sweden, Africa, and Norway. These people had written to me while I was on death row, and some had even come to visit me. They ended up becoming my extended family. They stood with me for years and fought the good fight. I don't know what would have happened to my mental state if it hadn't been for all the love and support that my European allies showed me. At the start, I didn't realize how vital that support would be.

From the moment of my arrest on a charge of multiple homicide, I'd maintained my innocence, refusing to believe the justice system would fail me, that the state could actually kill me for a crime I did not commit. There were others who agreed, most recently Pamela Colloff of *Texas Monthly* magazine, who had written a moving exposé on my case.

On this day, I sat at my metal writing table, responding to a letter Pamela had written me requesting information for a follow-up article she was preparing about my case. "They're either going to have to kill me or set me free," I wrote. "But if they kill me, the whole world's gonna know that Texas pumped poison in the veins of an innocent man."

I was three-quarters of the way through this letter, scribbling desperate words, when a guard approached my cell.

"Graves, come on," the voice boomed, his words echoing off the cell walls. "I've got orders to bring you out."

I was immediately on alert. This was jail, of course, where inmates don't exactly come and go for any old reason. I had learned by then that some officers weren't to be trusted.

"Can you tell me where we're going?" I asked, but the officer gave no explanation. It didn't feel right. He seemed to be withholding information, and I knew from all my time on death row that being brought to the front offices was a big deal: something either very good or very bad had happened. I hadn't heard from my attorneys that day, but I knew there was ongoing activity concerning my case.

"I'm not going anywhere without my attorneys," I said, letting the guard know that after years of being jerked around in the system, I knew good and well that *Gideon v. Wainwright* entitled me to counsel. My nervousness grew as we turned the corner and came to a large steel door with the words INTERROGATION ROOM written across the top.

Sensing my discomfort, the officer dispensed with whatever game he'd been playing. I would later find out that he knew the news I was about to receive, and he was just as nervous as I was. He opened the door quickly, revealing two members of my legal team, Nicole Cásarez and Jimmy Phillips Jr., and another officer, Sergeant Kuhn.

Nicole had been a great champion of justice in my case. In a search for more meaningful work, she'd given up a corporate legal career to become a journalism teacher at the University of St. Thomas in Houston. In 2002, she and her students heard about my case during a visit from David Dow, a University of Houston Law Center professor and founder of the Texas Innocence Network, the state's oldest innocence project. Nicole and her students had immediately volunteered to help with my case, and took on the role with gusto. In 2006, she became an official member of my legal team. Now, she looked as though she was holding back tears when she asked me how I was doing.

"I'm fine, Nicole. What's going on?" I knew that if I was going to get answers from anyone, it would be from her.

"Do you remember how you told me that God was good, when you were trying to lift my spirits about all of this?" she asked.

Of course I remembered saying those words, I told her; after all, holding tight to that belief had gotten me through some dark times on death row when I thought that the State of Texas might just succeed in killing me.

"You're going home, Anthony," Nicole said, her eyes growing wider as she spoke. "Siegler just dropped all the charges, and not only that, but she's willing to tell the world that you're actually innocent of this crime."

I didn't know what to say or do. I had just gotten the news that I had fought for, without letup, for nearly two decades. I'd gone into that room with my sword and my shield, my defenses up and ready to fight, but it appeared that the battle was already won. I thought for a brief moment that my lawyers might have misunderstood the prosecutor, Kelly Siegler, or that I might have misheard Nicole when she relayed the news. I had seen plenty of men pulled out of prison and put right back in when one court or another decided to reinstate, or allow reprosecution of, their cases. I had seen the courts take them on an emotional roller-coaster ride, their freedom dangled precariously in front of them before the state ripped away their last remaining hope. My own hopes had been dashed time and again. I feared that if I let myself believe the news was real this time, I might not be able to recover if justice was once again snatched from my tired fingers.

But then Sergeant Kuhn confirmed what Nicole had been saying. "Graves, do you want to go get your property?"

As the sergeant and I began to walk down the quiet hallway, it started to dawn on me: it's over. Several minutes later, a forty-five-year-old man with only a small box of possessions to my name—a few books, the legal papers that had helped me win my freedom, the photographs that were all I'd had of home—walked out of the living nightmare that had consumed my entire being for so long and into a new life that I hadn't prepared myself to start living. I had just made commissary, but getting my hands on that pittance of money would take time I wasn't prepared to give. "I want to get out of here before they change their damn minds," I said.

Once outside the jail, I embraced my lawyers and tasted the sweetness of freedom for the first time since a Brenham police officer had arrested me more than eighteen years before.

For all the years the wheels of justice had churned so slowly in my case, now there had hardly been time to make arrangements concerning my release. Even Nicole hadn't let herself believe the state was serious about dropping the charges until she'd got to the jail. Like me, she'd wanted to get the release process over with as quickly as possible. There was no ceremonial proceeding with a judge admonishing the state or apologizing for the system's treatment of me, nor were there any local news teams there to cover my release. It was only by pure coincidence that a crew from CBS's *48 Hours* was visiting that day, filming a documentary on my innocence claim.

I had only one thing on my mind as I prepared to get in the car and leave behind 6,640 days of pure hell in those jail cells. Richard Schlesinger, the reporter from *48 Hours,* looked at me and knew just what that was.

"Anthony, does your mom know?" he asked. It had all happened so fast that Momma had yet to hear the news.

"How about we call her?"

Nicole dialed the number and handed me a smartphone, an alien device developed and redeveloped many times over during the time I'd been locked up.

"Hello, Momma," I said as I prepared to ask her the question I had asked at the conclusion of every one of my conversations with her from jail. "What you cooking tonight?"

She wasn't used to getting a call from Nicole and then having my voice come on the line. She started to answer, but I had to interrupt her, the gravity of my words hitting me: "Well, that's good. Because I'm coming home, Momma."

PART ONE

THE ARREST

*I have walked that long road to freedom. I have tried not to falter;
I have made missteps along the way. But I have discovered the
secret that after climbing a great hill, one only finds that there are
many more hills to climb. I have taken a moment here to rest,
to steal a view of the glorious vista that surrounds me, to look back
on the distance I have come. But I can rest only for a moment,
for with freedom come responsibilities, and I dare not linger,
for my long walk is not ended.*

—NELSON MANDELA,
Long Walk to Freedom

AUGUST 18, 1992:
A FAMILY IS GONE

. . . . .

FOR ME, THE NIGHT of the crime was like any other night. I was just a few weeks shy of my twenty-seventh birthday, and I was dating a young woman named Yolanda Mathis. Our evening started at the home of her dad, Bubba, in Brenham, my hometown, about thirty-five miles south of Somerville, along Highway 36 in central Texas. Bubba's girlfriend Bernice had agreed to babysit Yolanda's eight-month-old daughter that night, so that Yolanda and I could have some time to ourselves. After Bernice got off work, we planned to head to my mother's apartment, where Yolanda and I would spend the night. It was the most convenient place we could go, since I had not yet found my own place after breaking up with a previous girlfriend four months prior. I wasn't serious enough with Yolanda to invite myself back to her place yet. In fact, I was staying a little bit of everywhere at this point in my life—a few nights with my brother, a few nights with my sister, a few nights at my mom's.

"Anthony, do you mind going to pick up Bernice from work?" Bubba asked at one point. He explained to me that another family member had borrowed his car but hadn't yet returned it, and Bernice, who worked at a nearby Sonic fast-food restaurant, would need a ride home after her shift. Bernice had been a babysitter for Yolanda when she was younger and now sat for Yolanda's daughter when we spent the night together, so I was happy to help out.

"Thanks," Bubba said. "Here's a couple of dollars for gas. She should be off work around ten thirty."

As I was leaving to pick Bernice up, Yolanda's younger brother and his girlfriend pleaded with me to take them to a Jack in the Box along the way. We decided to use the drive-thru window. I immediately recognized the attendant, a woman related by marriage to one of my younger sisters.

"Hey, Mary, I think we ought to get some burgers for free," I said, only half-joking. My request denied, we ordered enough food for the three of us and for Yolanda, who had stayed at home with the baby. We made it to Sonic just as Bernice was walking out the door. She hopped into the backseat and we headed back to Yolanda's dad's. We arrived there shortly before eleven and socialized for about thirty minutes. In the days to come, the timing and details of this night would take on far more importance than they ever should have had.

Before we left Bubba's house, I placed a call to my younger brother Arthur and asked him to make up a bed for me and Yolanda on the floor of my mother's front room. Her apartment was small, so we made do with modest sleeping arrangements. Yolanda was a good sport about this when I know she didn't have to be.

It was eleven thirty when Yolanda and I made it to my mother's, fast food in hand. While years later I would be forced to consider my final meal, I remember too well what might be called the first meal of my mounting mess: Yolanda had the Ultimate Cheeseburger with extra mayonnaise. I'd opted for a steak sandwich.

My sister Dietrich and brother Arthur were still awake when we arrived. I'm the eldest of five siblings. My sister Demetria, who was twenty-four at the time, and my brother Derrick, who was twenty-three, both lived nearby—Demetria in Austin with her husband and two children, and Derrick just twenty miles south in a small town called Bellville—and they visited often. Nineteen-year-old Dietrich and eighteen-year-old Arthur still lived at home with my mom in Brenham, and it was not uncommon to come home to a gathering like this. I opened the door to see Dietrich standing in the kitchen. Knock-kneed and tired, she was preparing fish sticks, not a gourmet creation but the only thing my mother had in her refrigerator at the time.

"What do you have in the bag?" she asked Yolanda as we came through the door with our Jack in the Box dinners.

"Go ahead and focus on those fish sticks," I teased, shooing her away. "Where's Arthur, anyway?"

She pointed to the back room, where I found my brother on the phone, cooing like one of those old-time Vegas crooners, singing to some girl on the other end. He laughed as he looked up to see me, knowing I had caught him in the act. He raised one hand to cover the phone and put his finger to his mouth as if to ask for quiet.

I offered him some of my steak sandwich as I started to sing, "Look at me, I'm as helpless as a kitten up a tree," mimicking Johnny Mathis loud enough for the woman on the other end to hear.

The next thing I knew, I was talking to her. She said her name was Kay and that Johnny Mathis was her favorite. We talked for a short time—mostly about nothing—before I handed the phone back to my brother and left the room, singing the Mathis tune at the top of my lungs. I reported back to the girls what I'd just seen and heard, and we shared a laugh at Arthur's expense.

The three of us talked until a little after midnight, when someone knocked at the apartment door. My sister answered, letting in a neighbor, Albert Wright. Albert had gone by the nickname Squeaky since we were little kids. Squeaky had come by to borrow some bread from my sister after getting a late-night urge to fry chicken. He also asked to use the phone. In the back room, Arthur let him make his call, after which Albert left with his two slices of bread. It was late, close to 2 a.m., when my sister finally retired to her room, giving me and Yolanda some privacy in the front room. We lay on a pallet on the floor, not expecting much more from our long day and late night; we had each other and some quiet now, and that was enough for us.

Little did I know that something horrible was happening that night some thirty miles from where we lay, something that would soon change everything for me.

News of the murders traveled quickly in the region, and it wasn't long until we got word about what happened. My sister Dietrich was the first to hear the grim details, learning about it early the next morning in a call from my aunt Chee Chee. She woke me up to remind me that my aunt needed a ride to work. I had been borrowing her car after mine was repossessed due to missed payments—a consequence of spending nights in the hospital with my oldest son, Terrell, then twelve years old, which I'd prioritized over holding small jobs to keep the car on the road. Terrell was born with sickle-cell anemia, and every time he got sick I'd be right there at the hospital with him. That was my main focus. My other two sons, Terrance (then nine) and Alex (then eight), luckily had not inherited the disease. But I was at the hospital often with Terrell. My aunt's car was what was getting me there at the time. Driving my aunt to work was part of the arrangement, and I knew Chee Chee was calling to make sure I wasn't running late.

"Did you hear what happened up in Somerville last night?" my sister asked in the way someone shares the latest gossip.

"No, what?" I asked.

"A family got murdered, and whoever did it put the house on fire."

I was still half-asleep, but replied that whoever committed a crime like that needed their ass kicked. I rolled back over next to Yolanda to squeeze the last few minutes of sleep out of the morning before telling her that we needed to pick up my aunt.

Meanwhile, fear and outrage were already beginning to choke the town of Somerville. With a population of just over fifteen hundred citizens, it was far from a hotbed of crime and had certainly never seen a murder of this magnitude. The whole town wanted justice, and justice meant holding someone—anyone—responsible for the act. The rush to identify the killer even infected the mayor, who came out in the papers the following day and stated that whoever committed the murders didn't deserve a trial. They should be caught and hanged, she insisted. That's the way law enforcement pursued the case.

In small towns like Somerville, funerals are communal events, and the local news reports provide abundant details. It had been a few days since the tragedy, and by now six caskets were laid out in the local gymnasium for all to see what had been done. Among the grievers was reported to be a man named Robert Carter, the father of one of the children murdered in the home. My family would soon come to realize that this was the same Robert Carter who had recently married our cousin Cookie. Carter showed up bandaged like a mummy, his head wrapped in white cloth as if to cover severe burns. The Texas Rangers took notice, and Carter instantly became a suspect. The Rangers followed Carter to his home after the funeral. When they asked if they could have a chat, he agreed. That chat turned into fourteen hours of interrogation at the local office of the Department of Public Safety.

No one knows exactly what was said during those fourteen hours, and I would never receive any notes or recordings taken during the interrogation, if any existed. The Rangers undoubtedly asked Carter why he'd shown up in bandages to the funeral of his burned child. They would question his odd reactions to it all. Above all, they would wonder whether he'd acted alone. What Carter said in his interrogation changed my entire life: he fingered me as his accomplice, placing me at the heart of a crime scene that I wouldn't have been able to find if my very life depended on it.

AUGUST 23, 1992:
FIVE DAYS AFTER THE MURDERS

· · · · ·

A KNOCK ON MY mother's front door disrupted the midmorning silence. It was her next-door neighbor Mike with news that made me uneasy.

"Hey, man, the police are looking for you," he said.

At first I didn't think I'd heard him right. We spoke for a few moments, and I thanked him for the information, then closed the door, perplexed.

My mind raced as I tried to figure out just what it might be about.

I put on a shirt and walked downstairs just in time to see a police cruiser pull up outside my mother's apartment. As I stood there out front, I immediately recognized the officer as a longtime veteran of the local force. The expression on his face as he approached was stern. His uniform gave his name: GARCIA.

"What's your name?" Officer Garcia asked.

"I'm Anthony Graves," I responded.

"Let's see some ID, Graves," he said.

I reached into my back pocket to retrieve my wallet and showed the officer my driver's license. He surveyed it, then explained that he had been ordered to pick me up and take me to the police station to answer some questions. Even though I wasn't under arrest at this moment, I felt like I had no choice, but that didn't bother me much as I had nothing to hide.

Mike, my mother's neighbor, had come outside to see what was happening, and by then Officer Garcia had asked me to put my hands behind my back. Cold and unforgiving steel pinched my wrists as my arms twisted into an uncomfortable and unfamiliar position.

"Officer, can you just tell me what's going on?" I pleaded.

8

"The officers will talk to you when we get to the station," he repeated.

I called out to Mike, asking him to tell my mom what had happened when she got home and to let her know I should be right back.

The ride through my hometown to the nearby Washington County Jail was quiet, except for when the cruiser radio came on. I heard nondescript voices mumbling, and I wondered how much of the conversation was about me. When we pulled up to a red light, another car pulled tight to our right. As I looked over, the driver peered into the squad car to see who was in the backseat. What must he have thought of me? It wouldn't be the last time I was paraded through town and put on display for all to see. My face began to burn with embarrassment and confusion. I still didn't know why I was being "taken downtown for questioning," in handcuffs no less, but I didn't imagine that the reason much mattered to the people watching my head bob above the window line of that cruiser.

Once inside the police station, I was led to the booking room, a window-less space with drab walls and chipping paint. Officer Garcia released the handcuffs and asked me to empty my pockets. I planted myself on a cold bench and placed on the countertop a pack of Certs, my wallet, my keys, and a broken silver chain.

"Can you tell me why I'm here?" I asked.

"Some Rangers are coming to talk to you. They'll let you know why you're here." I was about to meet the Texas Rangers, the division of Texas law enforcement based out of Austin, who had statewide jurisdiction to investigate crimes. Apparently the local officers had some help on this one.

A parade of impressively uniformed authorities walked in and out of the room, ignoring my requests for information. At least twenty minutes passed before four Texas Rangers and a magistrate walked into the booking room and turned their attention to me.

"Are you Anthony Graves?" one of the Rangers asked. That question had suddenly become a familiar one and a little more unsettling than when it was asked the first time that morning.

"Yes, sir, that's me," I said.

The Ranger ordered me to stand up. When I stood, the magistrate began to speak, catching me by surprise.

"You have the right to remain silent," she said bluntly. "Anything you say can and will be used against you. You have the right to an attorney. If you cannot afford one, then one will be appointed to you."

I listened, my concern mounting, as the magistrate continued to read me my rights. I heard the words coming from her mouth, but nothing she said answered the question of why I was there in the first place.

"You have been charged with capital murder," the magistrate continued. "You have no bond."

"Capital murder?" I asked flatly, as something like vertigo began to take hold. "Who? Me?" I stuttered, struggling to believe what I had just been told, repeating the word "who" in a punch-drunk stupor. The officer assured me that I'd have a chance to talk to other officers when they arrived.

"Man, you guys are making a big mistake. I've never even shot a gun in my life!" I said, not knowing that the actual crime had involved a hammer, a knife, a gun, and some gasoline. I responded that way because I heard the word "murder," and to me that implied a gun, but I had no idea what they were actually talking about. I urged the officers to reconsider, wanting to believe that as soon as they realized it was all an honest misunderstanding, everything would be OK.

．　．　．　．　．

While the historic 1966 ruling in *Miranda v. Arizona* required that police read a person his or her rights before questioning them in custody, by no means did Miranda guarantee due process for an accused man seeking justice. In practice, the rules on the street are made by the cops, definitely not by the arrested, and not even by the courts. Reading me my rights was not enough to ensure that all the *i*'s had been dotted and the *t*'s crossed.

I signed a document the magistrate presented to me saying I had been read those rights. This would protect police and embolden prosecutors in case I happened to say something stupid in the days leading up to a trial. I proceeded to pace back and forth across the booking room, as if movement might awaken me from this bad dream. The officers watching me tap myself repeatedly on the side of the head as I tried to make sense of it all probably thought I was crazy. My thoughts raced as my mind flooded with fear and disbelief. How could law enforcement just come to my mother's apartment and take me to jail for something I had nothing to do with?

"Mr. Graves, would you like to talk to us?" a Ranger finally asked. Of course I would, I told him. He led me out of the booking room and down a hall, his hand on my back as we turned a corner and walked to the interrogation room.

Up to that point, I had been treated like a criminal, but I hadn't yet been treated like a violent criminal. I learned the difference quickly.

Lift up your shirt. Turn around. The orders were delivered harshly and fast.

"What are those spots on your back?" one Ranger asked.

"It's just a skin fungus," I assured them. Later I would understand that they had been looking for burn marks. I learned then that little things that might otherwise seem meaningless can take on a life of their own in a murder investigation. The slightest burn might have confirmed for them my guilt. Eventually, a Ranger ordered me to take a seat. I still was not in handcuffs, which may have been another police tactic to make me relax and start confessing what they wanted to hear, even though I couldn't say what I didn't know.

"You might as well tell us everything," he said. "Robert has already told us, and he's putting everything on you."

"Robert who?" I responded. It was the first time I had heard the name of the man who had implicated me in this heinous crime.

"You know Robert," the Ranger said.

"Sir, I know several Roberts," I replied.

"Robert Carter," one of the officers offered after a pause. I didn't immediately recognize the last name. "Carter . . . Carter . . . Carter," I repeated to myself. Suddenly it dawned on me. I remembered a conversation between my mom and sister. My second cousin Cookie had recently married a young man named Robert Carter. Relief washed over my face as I smiled on the inside. If we were talking about the same guy, then surely this would all be cleared up soon. "That guy doesn't even know me," I told the Rangers. "Are you sure he said Anthony Graves?"

"He said your name," one of the Rangers responded. "And he told us all that you did it."

"I don't believe him," another added. "I think he's lying. I believe *he* did it, but I need you to tell us everything that happened."

I didn't know what to think. Here, members of the Texas Rangers had just told me that a man being held for the murder of six people had put the crime on me. But they also said that they didn't believe him. They wanted information from me that I did not have. All I could tell them was the truth.

"Sir, I don't know anything about him, and he doesn't know me," I said. "Ask that man anything about me. He can't even tell you my nickname on the streets!"

Lieutenant Earl Pearson was a tall, light-skinned black man who I guessed was in his late forties or early fifties. He towered over the room and carried himself as if he knew it. About an hour into the interrogation, one of the Rangers asked whether I'd be more comfortable speaking to Pearson.

"Sir, no one has to go anywhere," I said. "I have nothing at all to hide from any of you."

"I'll tell you what, Graves," he responded. "We're going to go out of the room and let you talk with the black Ranger." I was taken aback by the casual way he said this. Of course, I'd recognized immediately that I was surrounded by a team of mostly white law enforcement officials, and I knew too well the reality of rural Texas and how race figured in the state's criminal justice system. Still, the Ranger's assumption that I would be more comfortable talking to Lieutenant Pearson because he was black took me by surprise, even though he was right. The four white Rangers left the room as Pearson began to talk.

"Son, you're in a lot of trouble, and the only way I can help you is if you tell me everything. Is it OK if I turn this recorder on?"

"Go ahead, you can turn it on," I replied. I hoped that Pearson would be sympathetic to my plight. "Sir, are you sure that this guy said my name? I'm telling you the truth—he doesn't even know me."

"He said your name," Pearson said in a fatherly tone, like the wise old black characters you see in movies advising white characters in trouble. "I want to help you, but you have to tell me everything. The state is going to go after the death penalty in this case, and you can help yourself out by co-operating with me." It was the first time I had heard mention of the death penalty and the first time in this case that I'd been offered something in exchange for compromising the truth. I assured the Ranger that I wanted to cooperate but that I didn't know anything about the crime.

"I'm willing to take a lie-detector test, a truth-serum test, or whatever test you want me to take," I told him determinedly.

He looked at me carefully, considering the offer. "Let me make a call and see if I can set up a lie-detector test," he said. "We'll have to take you down to Houston to get it done."

The Rangers arranged with the local jailer to put me in a holding cell while the folks in Houston set things up.

The cell was quiet, and I waited there alone. Once the steel door shut behind me, I could see no one and no one could see me. The cell was small, maybe eight feet by ten feet, with dull, neutral walls. A small security window had been cut into the door so that officers doing their security checks could open the door to the pan hole. I was surprised by how well the cell shut out the notorious Texas summer heat. I felt like I'd been placed in a large freezer, with nothing but a cheap, thin blanket made of rough fabric and a plastic pillow that was as comfortless as the cell. Like most everything else in the cell, the bunk was made of hard, cold metal as cold as the floor. I sat on the bed, waiting for someone to come get me. It was my first experience with solitary confinement.

The time spent alone was disorienting; it was difficult to keep track of time. A couple of hours must have passed when I heard the slot in my door open and an officer call my name.

"Graves, come over here so I can put these handcuffs on you," he said. "They're here to get you."

I was eager as I placed my hands to the slot, almost numb to the touch of steel on my skin after spending the last few hours in an icebox. I just wanted to take the polygraph test and get this over with. I had plans with Yolanda that night, and I wasn't one to break a date.

The voice behind the steel door belonged to the local jailer. He wasn't one of the Rangers who had been interrogating me. He was from Somerville, where the crime had taken place. At more than six feet tall, he towered over me. He must have weighed three hundred pounds, or so his stature suggested. His uniform fit tightly, his big gut straining the buttons of his shirt. On the top of his head was a large cowboy hat that proclaimed him ready for action.

As the local jailer opened the cell door, Officer Lou Larson made his introduction by roughly grabbing hold of my arm. I remember thinking that he wasn't going to be easy to get along with. The sun was still shining as we left the building, but I could tell that quite a bit of time had passed since I'd been taken in for interrogation. Larson had pulled his patrol car up to the curb as close as he could get to the front door. Jerking me to the right side of the cruiser, he opened the back door. I slid into the backseat and settled in for the ride to Houston, seventy-five miles away. Officer Larson sped down Highway 290 at what felt like ninety miles per hour.

We arrived at Houston's Department of Public Safety only to find the parking lot empty. This shouldn't have been surprising given that it was a Sunday afternoon, but it caught me off guard. Officer Larson spoke through his radio to someone who must have had access to the building. A Ranger emerged to escort me inside. The scene was serious, but I wasn't nervous. The only reason I was there was because I wanted to cooperate fully with the investigation. I wanted all the authorities to know that. I desired vindication, for the officers and Rangers to acknowledge my innocence after a successful polygraph test. The way I envisioned it, I would pass muster with no problem, everyone would apologize for the inconvenience, and they'd take me home.

A Ranger led me into the room where I would test the ability of a machine to determine if someone was telling the truth. Once in the polygraph room, Officer Larson removed the handcuffs from my wrists in what was likely another police tactic to ease me into some confession, any confession. Operating the machine was a black man who must have been pushing sixty. He greeted me pleasantly. I felt comfortable with him, just as I had with Lieutenant Pearson. I thought that, being black, he would understand my situation—that we always seem to get caught up in the system despite what the evidence shows. I smiled at him as he offered a handshake. "How are you doing today?" he asked as we exchanged pleasantries better suited to a ballpark than the innards of a police station.

He told me his name, and he billed himself as little more than a modest test administrator. I didn't know at the time that he too worked for the Rangers and that his easygoing approach was part of a larger plan to make me comfortable enough that I might talk.

As the polygraph operator explained the test, his instructions were clear and direct.

"Make sure you respond only with a yes or no answer," he admonished.

At the Ranger's request, I sat down in a hard chair that faced a closed door. He attached clips tightly to my fingers and affixed a complex contraption to my chest. His questions were simple and relentless. I was mystified as he continued, asking the same questions in as many different ways as he could.

Q: *Were you involved in killings of the Davis family?*
A: *No.*
Q: *Were you at the home of the Davis family when they were murdered?*
A: *No.*
Q: *Is your name Anthony Graves?*
A: *Yes.*
Q: *Is Anthony Graves your name?*
A: *Yes.*
Q: *Did you murder the Davis family?*
A: *No.*

As he administered the test, the Ranger had positioned himself behind me, where my peripheral vision could pick up only the slightest glimpse of him. I had wanted to see his reaction as I answered the questions, to gauge whether he believed me or, more importantly, whether the machine did. I heard its clicks and zips and hums as it made its strange recordings.

The test lasted nearly fifteen minutes. I was relieved to be done, to have the questions stop. I hadn't made any mistakes, answering in a clear yes or no to everything I'd been asked. Now, I thought, these people can apologize and get me back home. During my interrogation at the Washington County Jail, I'd told the police where I was on the night of the murders and who was with me and at what specific times. Curiously, the lie-detector test never addressed whether I had an alibi; it sought only a yes or no, never an explanation. Later, I would recall this as an odd omission, but I would come to realize that no one cared about my alibi, or my fate. They wanted someone to blame, and here I was.

The Ranger removed the clasps from my fingers.

"Well, I can finally go home now," I said to him with a smile.

He furrowed his brow as the edges of his mouth turned down slightly. "Not so fast," he said. "You didn't pass the test."

"How did I not pass the test?" I asked in disbelief.

"You failed, son."

My heart sank. I'd come to Houston eager to prove to the Rangers I was telling the truth, but I quickly realized they were not interested in the facts.

I would understand later that the test had been a sham, designed to manipulate me into making a false confession. Their past experience in law enforcement had taught the officers that if I believed I had failed a lie-detector test, I might be more likely to tell the Rangers what they wanted to hear.

On cue, it seemed, the Rangers seized their chance. Six uniformed agents piled into the polygraph room, like ants pouring from a newly kicked cone. They escorted me into another room. There, they became aggressive.

I was seated at a large steel table in a room just big enough to accommodate the Rangers surrounding me, who demanded that I admit my involvement in the crime. From every angle, officers charged in and out of my personal space, one getting so close I could feel his breath on my skin. Up to that point, I'd been composed. Finally, I broke, tears of frustration rushing uncontrollably down my cheeks. It was at this point that Ranger Miller, one of the authorities who had driven down separately from Brenham to the Houston facility, instructed the others to leave the room.

"I just want to have a little private conversation with Mr. Graves," he told them. I would later come to recognize his maneuver as part of the Good Cop, Bad Cop routine frequently dramatized in the movies. In this song and dance, one officer uses scare tactics to shake your resolve and frighten you. Another pretends to come to your rescue, swooping in at the last possible moment to relieve the manufactured tension.

"I drove all the way down here just so I could talk with you, Graves," he said, summoning a friendly and understanding demeanor. The change in tone was a welcome respite, but again, it was just part of the game. Later I would see it as an effort to solicit my gratitude by confessing.

By then I was confused, shaken by their tactics, and visibly distraught. The tears that covered my face weren't just in response to the trauma of that interrogation. They were, in part, a delayed response to Officer Larson's manhandling. When the officers came into the polygraph operator's room after the test, Larson had grabbed me by my right arm and twisted it so far behind my back, I thought he was going to break it. I was literally on tiptoe trying to ease some of the pain as he ushered me forcefully out of the room. Then, too, Ranger Miller had appeared out of nowhere to interrupt Officer Larson's aggressive tactics. I was angry that they were treating me like a guilty man, like they truly believed I'd committed that heinous crime. My mounting disorientation gave Ranger Miller the slight opening through which he jammed his oversized cowboy boot.

"Graves, let's try to do this again," he said in a reassuring voice. "Listen, son, you are in serious trouble here, and I want to help you. But you have to cooperate with me. Just tell me what Carter did."

"I don't know what he did because I wasn't there," I said yet again, fighting a sense of despair. I felt like I was banging my head against a wall.

"You're just going to let him get away with putting everything on you?" he asked.

I hesitated for a moment, tasting the salt from my tears. With the accusations mounting, I knew that I needed to collect myself.

"Sir, I don't know why this man lied on me," I started. "I don't know anything about this crime, and quite frankly, I'd rather you caught the person who did that to those people."

After a while, with Good Cop Miller's attempts to pull a false confession out of me yielding nothing new, some of the other Rangers, including Ray Coffman, the lead investigator on the case, returned to the room.

My interrogation lasted well into the night; it was nearly two in the morning when they finally relented. I had eaten nothing and had only a few sips of water, and nothing was ever offered since I'd arrived for another round of police tactical maneuvering. They wanted me weak to break me under their pressure. Ranger Coffman walked up to me and looked me in the eyes. "Graves," he declared, "I don't believe you did this. But if you don't give me anything on Carter, then we're going to put this whole thing on you. And if you're telling the truth, then don't let no grass grow on your grave." I wondered if he appreciated the irony of his words.

"I don't know anything about this crime, and I don't know this man," I repeated.

"Have it your way, Graves," Ranger Coffman said. "Go ahead, Larson. Take him back and lock him up."

AUGUST 23, 1992:
BURLESON COUNTY JAIL

· · · · ·

INSTEAD OF GOING BACK TO the Washington County Jail in Brenham, I was taken to a different jail in Milam, a neighboring county about sixty miles north of my hometown. Officer Larson only knew one speed, and he drove it on our way north.

When we arrived, I immediately asked to use the phone. I knew my mom was probably out of her mind with worry. Officer Larson gave the on-duty local officer the OK for me to make a call. I felt an instant sense of relief hearing the phone keys beep as I pressed each number.

"Hello?" she answered wearily, since it was after 3 a.m., and she was worried sick about me.

"Hey, it's me," I said.

"Boy! Where in the world you at?" Her voice held a combination of panic and relief.

"These police got me in some small town in Milam County," I explained. "I don't know what's going on."

"What? Why in the hell are they arresting you?" she asked, her voice rising. She wasn't making me feel any better, but I didn't expect her to. I could feel the tension rising in my own voice as I told her what I had gathered from the day's events. "They say that Cookie's husband said I did the crime in Somerville with him," I told her.

"You don't even know him," she said, the same response I'd given under questioning by the police.

"I know, Momma. That's what I've been trying to tell them. They had me in Houston all day asking me about this crime."

"You don't even know Bobbie and 'em!" she yelled, referring to the Davises. "Why would that boy put you in this mess?"

I didn't know, and I didn't know what to tell her. All I knew, from what I could piece together from the various Rangers grilling me, was that Robert Carter had decided to lie. The reality began to hit me that I was going to have to spend at least some time in jail while the mess got sorted out. It was hard to accept that someone's lies alone were enough to hold me there.

My mother tried to reassure me. She believed, like me, that the Rangers couldn't pin a crime on me that I knew nothing about. They certainly wouldn't be able to do it on the word of Robert Carter alone. Perhaps my mom had convinced herself of that over the course of what had to have been a very long day, carrying over to the darkest hours of morning. I'd learn that her neighbor Mike had told her what happened. She had gone so far as to call the police station in an effort to find out what was going on. I wasn't surprised to learn that they wouldn't tell her anything.

"Man, Momma, this is a crazy nightmare," I said. I asked about Yolanda. Mom told me she hadn't seen her. And then our time was up.

"Hopefully this will all be over by tomorrow," I said. "I'll call you the first chance I get."

"All right, son," she replied, her voice trembling. "Don't you worry. They can't put nothing on you like this."

A jailer escorted me to an empty cell, closed off from the rest of the facility. There were other cells, communal cells, even, where people waited together for their appearances in court. But again I found myself in solitary confinement; a steel door closed behind me with the pan lid covered so that I couldn't look out. It was almost dawn. I sat there with only my thoughts, a thin blanket, and a plastic pillow, trying to make sense of it all. But I was too physically and mentally exhausted to make much progress.

Eventually I drifted to sleep on the butcher-block bed. A few hours later, a jailer and a jail trusty woke me up with breakfast. Trusties, also known as porters, are inmates assigned various tasks along the jailhouse runs, the walkways that stretch in front of a row of cells. It's considered a privilege to be able to mop, sweep, and buff these runs, partly because of the freedom of movement it provided and partly because everyone could see you move around while they were locked in their cells with no place to go. In some jails, the trusties look out for other inmates, helping them pass notes and such. This particular trusty asked if I wanted a broom and mop to clean out my cell. His question suggested that he thought I might be there long enough to call the place home. I had no such plans.

"Nah, man, I don't need that," I told him. "But say, could you ask the jailer if I could use the phone?" The trusty didn't seem interested in my question, so I asked another.

"Any chance you can let me have a cigarette?"

"Let me see if I can find you one," he said. "But I'm not supposed to give you nothing." He leaned closer as his voice dipped to a whisper. "Look, dude. I don't know what you've done, but they told us not to talk to you and not to pass you anything."

I wasn't sure how to take his response. Why were they keeping me in isolation?

"I'll try to get you one," he continued. "But don't let them catch you smoking it."

I thanked him as I noticed a jailer approaching my cell. I called out to him about needing a phone.

"Sure, I'll get it back here for you," the jailer told me.

Fifteen minutes passed before the trusty returned with a cigarette and slid it through the small slot in my door. He was discreet as he gave me a light. I took the cigarette between my fingers and brought the stiff paper end to my lips. I puffed once and inhaled deeply.

"Thanks, man," I said. "I appreciate this, big time."

"No problem," he said with a nod before making a quick exit, not wanting to be seen talking with me. Hours passed as it became clear that no one was going to bring me a phone.

I was growing increasingly frustrated and angry. I wanted to talk to my mother again; I needed to vent about this situation that I had to believe would be straightened out at any moment. But a few hours later—and still with no phone call home—an officer came to move me to another jail. My situation seemed only to be getting worse.

At the new jail, I was put in the showers for sanitizing, and as I undressed, the officers asked to take all my clothes. Apparently they wanted to test what I was wearing for traces of evidence connecting me to the murders, despite those horrific events being more than five days ago now. I gave them all I was wearing, as I would do anything to help them solve their case and get me back home. After the shower that did little to make me feel clean, I was given a new uniform. It looked like a Halloween costume.

They'd scrapped the traditional black-and-white stripes in favor of an orange getup. The black letters across the back told everyone that I was a ward of Burleson County, which is where I was headed, apparently.

"We're transporting you to another jail," Officer Larson explained, his tone no different than it had been the day before. "It won't take us but thirty minutes." I wondered to myself whether those thirty minutes took into account Officer Larson's now notorious driving. He slapped handcuffs to my wrists, their grasp tightening with each click, then collected my personal property from the main desk and stuffed it in a bag, escorting me back to the same police car I'd gotten acquainted with the night before. It was another sunny day, hot, as if the Texas summer was making its last stand. All I could think about was going home. I didn't know where I was being taken, or why, but I was hopeful that the mess would be sorted out that day. Looking back, I find it remarkable that it still hadn't occurred to me that I should have an attorney. It may sound naive, but I still believed my innocence would be enough to see me through.

The Burleson County Jail, located in the town of Caldwell, looked like an old Victorian-style house and was the old Caldwell jail. Off-white stone rose high above the ground, culminating in rounded pillars like those of the state's famous painted churches. Meals were cooked in a small adjoining house and walked over to the jail by the jailer on duty. The day we arrived, the gravel parking lot was mostly empty. Officer Larson led me inside to the head jailer.

"Here's Graves," Larson said. "All you have to do is book him in and place him in his cell." I couldn't help thinking that he had described me like a dog being dropped off for boarding by someone about to go off on a weekend getaway. I followed the new jailer into what might have been a front living room but served as the booking office. A surge of voices collided with a clanging sound, disrupting the silence. I traced the source of the noise to the loudspeakers in the office. I realized that I was hearing a mass of jumbled conversations coming from different jail cells. It was hard to make out what the inmates were saying. It was even harder to determine which cells the noises were coming from.

The booking formalities done, the jailer placed me in cell number 2. Though the jail was small, it was packed. It felt like a scene from a high school cafeteria, with each person outshouting the next until the noise reached an indecipherable buzz. Adding to this commotion was a television, way down the hall, and a loud fan that rattled helplessly against the oppressive August heat.

My personal quarters were as I'd come to expect: there was a bed with worn-out springs holding a lumpy mattress that looked like it had seen more than its share of inmates. In the back of the cell was a small window. An intercom speaker was mounted in the wall next to the cell door. I was taking in my dismal new surroundings when I heard somebody call out my name.

"Yo! Graves! This is Scotty Burns," an inmate yelled from another cell.

"Who?" I asked, loud enough for him to hear me.

"It's Scotty Burns. From Brenham."

I peered through the bars of the door, scanning the other cells. It shouldn't have surprised me to see someone from home in jail. Guys were always getting picked up for one thing or another. Just about everyone, it seemed, went in and out of custody as a fact of life. But still, to find Scotty, an acquaintance from home, in an adjacent cell in Caldwell, threw me for a loop.

But it was the man in head bandages in the cell across the way that drew my attention. Without his mummy wrap, I'd have had a hard time picking him out of a lineup. But in that moment, I was sure it was Robert Carter. Every hair on my body stood at attention.

I stared at him for a while, trying to glean from his face something, anything, that could help me understand why he'd put me there. Finally, I decided to engage him.

"Say, man," I called out to him. "Do you really think I did this with you?" As I waited for his response, part of me wondered if Carter might be crazy. He didn't speak. He just shook his head as if to say no and raised his index finger to his lips, urging me to hush.

"For my momma's sake and for my kids', will you please tell these people the truth?" I pleaded.

He nodded at me before walking slowly from the front of his cell door. Carter's response was at once maddening and comforting. The odds of a cell being available directly across from him seemed long. They had put me there, I was sure, believing I would talk to him if given the chance. My head shook with red-hot emotion while the blood in my body ran cold.

"Look out, Graves. They got them speakers on in the cells!" It was Scotty Burns again, hollering at the top of his lungs. His news wasn't news to me.

"Shit, Scotty. I don't give a damn. I want them to hear me so I can go home!" I retreated into my cell, determined to keep my emotions in check.

I feared what might happen if I didn't get a grip on myself. Besides, Carter had just assured me that he would tell the truth. I comforted myself with the thought that as soon as that happened, they'd surely let me go, probably as early as the next morning.

Just as I'd started to calm myself with that thought, another voice called out.

"Two cell! Look out, two cell!"

"What's up?" I responded. The small window in the back wall of my cell faced the jail's driveway. I couldn't see my neighbors from there, but I found it was easier to hear them. Positioned against this back wall, I told him my name and he told me his. Kevin was one of two young men in the cell next to mine.*

I could tell by the tone of their voices that they were scared. Kevin told me that he'd never been in jail before. He'd been driving his girlfriend's car and, unbeknownst to him, there were drugs in the trunk. The police released the girl but arrested Kevin and his friend.

"What do you think they'll do to us?" he asked, not concealing his fear. "Have you ever been arrested before?"

I told them they'd be all right. They didn't own the car, after all, and the cops didn't find any drugs on them. But Kevin's questions took me aback. I was concerned about him and his friend, but I was really trying to reassure myself. Kevin's doubt in the system raised fresh feelings of doubt in me. There were many things that I could have told him about my own experience with Texas law enforcement, but I didn't. I could've told him that I first got familiar with the criminal justice system a few years beforehand, when I was twenty-two. I hadn't been a big-time drug dealer, but you didn't have to be a ringer for the cartels to catch the attention of police at the height of the War on Drugs. I made a few hundred bucks a month selling marijuana, but one of my sales was to an undercover agent. A month later, the police arrested me for possession with the intent to distribute.

I thought I'd just be given a fine, since I had no record and had sold only a small amount of dope. By the time the police got ahold of me, though, the charge had changed. They accused me of possession of a controlled

---

* Though the names in this memoir are real to the best of my memory, this inmate's name has been altered for privacy.

substance with intent to distribute, a cocaine charge that I knew nothing about. I learned early in life that the system has a way of turning nothing into something when it wants to. I sat in jail on a $45,000 bond. The district attorney offered me a deal that he'd offered many others—plead guilty, and you'll serve 180 days in jail; go to trial, he said, and you may have to pay the trial tax. He assured me that if I went before a jury, I would serve fifteen years in prison. I was helpless and voiceless. The prosecutor was precise and his voice was cutting. It was his best offer, and I didn't want to chance turning it down. Like so many, I took the deal, falsely confessing to the cocaine charge. It wasn't worth the risk of spending most of my adult life in prison.

I could have tried to reassure Kevin that the truth would prevail. I also could have told him, from my experience, that he was in for a ride, even on the simplest of drug charges. The best I could muster was a sentence or two of encouragement. I needed to hear for myself that everything would be all right. I had compromised the truth once before in this system, but with my life on the line, there was no way I was going to do it again.

AUGUST 25, 1992:
THE GRAND JURY

. . . . .

THE STATE MOVED QUICKLY in the days after my arrest as they prepared their case against me. During the last week of August—a little over a week after the Davis family murders—there was a grand jury proceeding. Yolanda, Bernice, and Bubba all testified on my behalf, trying to convince the jurors and prosecutor the truth regarding my whereabouts on the night of the crime, but apparently their words fell on deaf ears. By the time the grand jury convened, I still did not have an attorney, focused as I was on two things only: the truth and going home. Further, beyond a rote reading of my Miranda rights during the stress of my arrest, no one from law enforcement had brought up the question of legal representation.

During this time, I hadn't had much contact with anyone in my family besides my mom. I didn't want my sons coming up to the jail and seeing me in an orange jumpsuit. Yolanda was the one other person I'd talked to during these first days in jail, but the jailhouse calls were so damn expensive, we'd quickly run up her father's phone bill and the phone got turned off for insufficient payment.

I marveled at how quickly I adjusted to jail in such a short time. I somehow managed to sleep a little better each night, despite merciless stabbings from bed springs that themselves seemed convinced of my guilt. That old lumpy mattress had proven just as uncomfortable as it looked, contorting my spine with a roller-coaster like dip in its center. Mosquitoes feasted on my weary skin in what seemed like a nightly ritual. Then again, maybe that sleep was just a mirage, because my mind and body certainly didn't feel rested.

On August 25, the jailer on duty approached my cell on a mission. He asked whether I had any interest in testifying before the grand jury. I jumped to my feet eagerly, scared that the offer might expire if I didn't act immediately. His next words brought instantaneous relief.

"Another officer will be by to escort you to the courthouse," he told me. "Wait for a few minutes." He handed me a bar of soap and a toothbrush. Even herculean attempts to keep a cell clean couldn't beat the filth brought on by late summer in the heart of Texas. I soaped up and scrubbed away a layer of sweat that had poured from me ceaselessly since they'd brought me to Caldwell. I rushed to get ready, still sure at this point that once somebody, anybody, heard my testimony, they'd send me home.

An officer slapped handcuffs onto my wrists, a sensation that was becoming familiar.

"We're just going to take a little walk," he told me. "Now don't you cause me any problems."

Did he think I'd try to make a run for it with the state's steel still strapped to my hands? I just nodded, and he led me to the courthouse, about three hundred yards from the jail, in the middle of the town square. A recognizable face greeted me as I entered. It was Ranger Earl Pearson.

"How are you, Ranger?" I asked.

"I'm fine, Graves. How're they treating you?"

"Not too bad," I assured him, thinking that most dog owners I knew wouldn't leave their dog in that old kennel they called a jail.

"I was told that you're willing to testify before the grand jury." His statement was more like a question. I told him I was more than willing.

"Do you have an attorney?" he asked. This was the first time anyone had raised this question. Maybe Ranger Pearson had taken a liking to me, or maybe he just felt pity.

"I don't need an attorney if I'm just going to tell the truth," I answered. I'd been taught in school that the United States had the best criminal justice system in the world. At the time, I wanted to believe that the system works. I *needed* to believe it would work for me this time, because so much was on the line. My life hung in the balance. Even though I'd falsely confessed once before, I did that in part because I had put myself in that situation. If I hadn't been trying to sell weed, I wouldn't have been in a position where they could put a false cocaine charge on me. It was my fault that time, and I rationalized accepting the plea deal because my own actions had put me in that spot.

Now, facing a capital murder charge for a crime I'd had no part in, the stakes were so much higher. I continued to believe that such an obvious error would be corrected. Of course they would come to see that I was totally innocent, that there wasn't any proof saying otherwise. After all, this charge carried the death penalty, so the state had to get it right, didn't it?

"I would appreciate if you were in there with me," I told Pearson.

"No problem. I'll go in there with you," he said.

The room was simple, adorned only with the Texan relics that decorate many of the state's courtrooms. Giant stars sent the message that the state meant business. I saw the grand jury members gathered around a table. A court stenographer sat patiently in front of a contraption that looked like the love child of a computer and a typewriter.

A petit jury—twelve people deliberating and deciding guilty or not guilty by a unanimous verdict in a criminal trial—is what most people think of when they imagine jury duty or see a jury portrayed on television. A grand jury, however, is basically a function of the district attorney's office. It's operated entirely by the DA, and there is no judge present (although I later learned you could go to a judge for a ruling if you had an attorney who opposed something that was happening in the grand jury).

The DA's office opens a felony case by seeking an indictment in the grand jury, in which a majority of the panel must vote by a show of hands whether there is probable cause to formally accuse a defendant of a crime. The grand jurors are an investigative body too and are allowed to directly question both witnesses and any defendant who chooses to testify at this early stage of the proceedings. In that way it's very unusual, as it's the only time in a criminal case when jurors can ask questions directly of witnesses, and then it's up to the jurors to decide if there's enough evidence to let the case continue. It's a low threshold, but an important one. The grand jury can also reject charges in what's known as a "no true bill" if jurors feel there isn't enough evidence to support an indictment. I, of course, wanted a no true bill in my case and held out hope for it given my innocence. I wanted to tell the grand jury, the state, and anyone else who would listen that I had nothing to do with the murders.

Burleson County's district attorney was Charles Sebesta. He was slender but imposing. With short, parted hair combed from left to right atop his head, wire-rimmed glasses, and a prominent nose, he looked the part of a serious Texas prosecutor. He acted the part, too, taking immediate control of the room. He seemed charged up for the proceedings, and later I would wonder if Sebesta's excitement stemmed from the fact that I'd shown up voluntarily and without an attorney.

"Graves, if you'll come in and have a seat right here, we can get this interview started," Sebesta said, his matter-of-fact tone commanding the attention of the grand jurors. "Will you state your full name?"

"Anthony Charles Graves."

"How old are you?"

"I'm twenty-seven years old."

Sebesta explained that the jury would be asking me questions. I could answer any or all of them.

"I don't have any problems answering your questions," I said.

One grand juror asked me my age. "Twenty-six," I said. Several grand jury members proceeded to ask about my involvement in the crime. Again, there wasn't much I could say. I hadn't been there. I couldn't tell them anything. All I could do was insist repeatedly on my innocence. Over time, their questions got more specific, each one seemingly lobbed at me with purpose.

"Have you ever owned a knife before?" one of the jurors asked.

"No," I answered simply, because I'd never owned a knife as a weapon. I wasn't thinking about the knife that, almost two years prior, a former employer and friend, Roy Allen, had given me as a souvenir, from a kit of cheap assembly knives he'd purchased. I hadn't seen that knife in more than a year, and I'd only ever "owned" it in the most superficial sense. I didn't realize it at the time, but this brief exchange would take on enormous significance to my case going forward. My answer, though truthful, was an unforced error that would come back to haunt me.

At some point during my prior questioning, before the grand jury proceeding, I had described to the police my whereabouts on the night of the crime. I gave them my alibi, which I thought would be pretty helpful for them to offer to the grand jury, particularly because it was truthful. I hadn't been allowed to observe any of Yolanda's, Bubba's, or Bernice's testimony—those proceedings were conducted in private. Even if I'd had a lawyer, she would not have been allowed in the room other than when I went in to testify, and then she would technically not be permitted to speak to the jurors but only to observe and whisper advice in my ear. I did learn that they never invited the testimony of Yolanda's brother or his girlfriend, who'd come with me to pick up Bernice that night. I had no idea why the state wouldn't want as much information as possible when someone's life was on the line. I'd heard it said that the grand jury is so much in a DA's control, a prosecutor could indict a ham sandwich if he or she wanted to. I wasn't impressed with control. I wanted the truth to come out. But my arrest and the legal proceedings were starting to look like some kind of a game.

Ultimately, their questions exhausted, the grand jury members ceded control back to Sebesta. He asked if I had anything further to say to them. I certainly did. I told the jury again that I had nothing to do with the crime. I told them, too, that I'd be glad to answer any questions they might have in the future. To my surprise, my words didn't seem to register. The jurors all shared the same emotionless expression, staring through or over me. I desperately wanted some morsel of recognition that I could cling to, but that never came. My mind went as blank as their faces.

I shared the short walk back to jail with the same officer who had escorted me the first time. On the way back, I saw Ranger Pearson. I nodded at him, the best I could do with my hands shackled. He waved back. My optimism rose. Back in my cell, I saw Carter looking out from his bars.

"Carter, I just testified in front of the grand jury," I said, approaching my cell door.

"That's good," he said. "They asked me to testify, but my attorney advised me not to go."

That Carter was already receiving legal advice had somehow eluded me, and it gave me pause. It is easy to look back and realize that, of course, Carter's attorney would tell him to clam up, as he'd had plenty to hide.

"But I'm going to do it," he continued. "So I can tell them the truth."

Relief poured over me as I let out a sigh.

"Thank you, man," I told him. "This is real hard on my mother."

I knew that they had held me on Carter's word alone. If he recanted his lie, they'd have to set me free. I prepared myself mentally to say good-bye to jail, to the vicious mattress springs that had become my nighttime nemesis.

The following morning, on August 26th, Carter went to see the grand jury. I was in my cell thinking about home when I heard the clicks and clangs as he was returned to the block after his testimony before the panel.

"Did you tell them the truth?" I asked.

"Yes, I did. My attorney told me they'll probably be releasing you soon. But they'll keep me."

Carter seemed sincere, and I'd later learn that he was telling the truth. He'd testified against the advice of his attorney, who had warned him that the questions could be tricky. Carter had indeed confirmed my innocence. When asked about the crime, he told the jurors that I'd had nothing to do with it.

He had just delivered the best news yet since my arrest. Still, I had nagging questions that I wanted to ask him. Had he really killed all those people? Did he light those children on fire? I looked intently at him through my cell door. I was scared. I knew that I was looking at the man who had gotten me into this mess. I didn't want to know that I was also looking into the face of a killer. I suppressed my curiosity and let it go. Carter had told the truth. I was ready to forgive him for his lie.

AUGUST 27, 1992:
THE LINEUP

. . . . .

EXCEPT FOR MY MOM, I'd had little communication with my family. I trusted that my sons' mothers knew me well enough to defend me to the boys, and I would learn much later that that had been the case. I was focused on making sure the truth got told so that I could go home. I thought that would be soon. Carter had assured me he'd told the truth to the grand jury and that he thought that would be enough for the state to dismiss the charges and let me go home. I waited and waited for the doors to open, for my name to be called and for someone to tell me to pack up my belongings.

The day after our grand jury testimonies, Carter was moved to another jail. With him gone, I was moved to a different cell at Caldwell. My new cellmate, Angel, had been there for a while and oozed practical jailhouse savvy. Angel was white, with a wrinkled, almost leathery face. His hair was cropped close to his scalp. He was sitting on the top bunk, reading a book, when I arrived. He didn't acknowledge me until I made the misstep of placing what little property I had on the bunk beneath him.

"I sleep on the bottom bunk, son," Angel said. "I just get up here to read." He shot me a disarming smile. "An old man like me can't be jumping down and up here every night."

I smiled back at him. It didn't take long for Angel to open up about the ins and outs of life at Caldwell.

If Angel didn't tell me everything he knew, it must have been close. I learned the tendencies of the various jailers. I listened closely as he described his personal survival strategy. It might have been titled "Getting What You Want." I liked him for his directness, assuming that that was

31

what I was getting. I had just begun to feel comfortable with Angel when his tone shifted from jovial to serious.

"Say, Graves, you didn't do this crime with that dude, did you?"

He was smooth. He wanted me to confide in him. I wanted nothing more than to prove my innocence.

But Angel was facing charges of racketeering; he was looking at sixty years or more. He was hoping to cut a deal with the DA, and if he got something out of me, that would be his chance. So Angel started sharing information with me about how things were done at Burleson County Jail. Helpful information. He opened up about his family, and before I knew it, we were talking like old friends. I don't think he'd counted on me being innocent, though.

"Nah, I didn't do it," I replied. "The guy doesn't really know me. For some reason, he just said my name."

"That's good to hear, son. You don't seem like that kind of guy, the kind that would go in and kill innocent children."

I told him I had children of my own. He told me he had grandchildren.

"You know what you ought to do, Graves?" he asked, turning serious. "You should write an affidavit with everything you did, starting the day before the crime. You ought to show it to the prosecutor."

My eyes lit up. Angel knew his way around the system. It seemed like a good idea.

I gave the affidavit my full attention. Angel made it easy for me, maybe too easy, as all he had to do was reach up to the top bunk to get pen and paper for me to start writing. I tried hard to remember everything I had done in the hours before, during, and after the time of the crime. While I had already given all this information to the Rangers and the grand jury, they hadn't seemed to listen to what I was saying. Maybe if I wrote it down and sent it to the DA, it would have more impact and finally be accepted as the truth.

After about thirty minutes of thinking and writing, I was satisfied that I had included a good amount of detail. Later I learned that the minutia is often what separates life from death in a capital case, and I had barely scratched the surface. I knew nothing about trace evidence, hair and fiber analysis, or the high value of a one-second discrepancy in a crime-scene timeline. But I also didn't know that my case would barely be investigated, once Carter had incriminated me. So, unaware of the recklessness of what I was doing, I asked to see the head jailer, Officer Burkhalter, who was almost cartoonish in his appearance.

"What's up, Graves?" he said.

"Sir, I just wrote out an affidavit," I said. "I'm trying to get it to the prosecutor."

"All right," he said flatly. "Give it to me and I'll get it to him today."

Thinking I had just possibly saved myself, I later learned this would turn out to be one of so very many disappointments. I never heard about the affidavit again.

Not long after, some Texas Rangers arrived at my cell door. They were there to conduct a lineup, they said. I still didn't have an attorney, and I still didn't think I needed one. From what little I knew about attorneys in criminal cases, they usually suggested that you take a plea deal no matter your innocence (which I was not about to do) and wanted a bunch of money up front (which I did not have). Granted, this was all learned conjecture from street talk around town growing up, but it contributed to my uninterest in legal representation. Despite or perhaps because of all this, I agreed to the lineup. In my naïveté, I thought it might work in my favor.

I didn't know much about lineups at the time. As it turned out, on the night of the Somerville murders, a witness had seen two men buying a can of gasoline at a local quick shop. Law enforcement was seeking a positive identification. I immediately sensed that something was off. I was astonished to see that the others in the lineup were merely boys. Most were between fifteen and seventeen years old and looked like the kids I used to play baseball with in high school. I was in my late twenties. It wasn't hard to see that I would stand out.

Each person in a lineup takes his place under a number. There were seven us, and they'd saved spot 4, the middle spot, just for me. Worse, I had to clink and clank my way to the designated spot in prison chains. A Ranger finally removed my handcuffs, but not before I'd made my first impression on the witness behind the glass. I'd wanted to believe that this was an opportunity for me to establish my innocence. Once in the actual lineup, however, it became clear that this was an effort to identify *me*, not an unbiased procedure meant to confirm the identity of someone the witness may have seen before.

I didn't believe there wasn't much else I could do, so I complied with their demands. The instructions were simple: Turn your head to the left. Turn to the right. Look straight ahead.

"All right, guys," I heard a Ranger say. "You can all go. Except for you, Graves."

I let out an audible puff of exasperation. It felt no different than when the Ranger had delivered the bad news about the lie-detector test a week prior. Still, some part of me remained hopeful. I knew I wasn't at that gas station. I knew it wasn't me.

"Graves, I have some bad news for you," one of the Rangers said. "That person behind the glass just picked you out of the lineup."

The sense of vertigo I'd previously experienced returned with a vengeance. *How is this happening?* My shock was palpable. I was also scared and angry. After having cooperated with the Rangers 110 percent, they'd put me in there as the only adult among a bunch of teenagers. I'd arrived in jail clothing while the others had on regular street clothes. There was one spot left open for me, position number 4, right in the center, which I would later learn is the "guilty" spot, the position most often chosen by witnesses. As I'd taken my place, still in handcuffs, I didn't know that the witness was already behind the one-way mirror, watching me the whole time. The resentment that had been building inside me since my arrest erupted in that moment.

"What? C'mon, man!" I exclaimed. "I've been cooperating with you all this whole time. Shit, man! I want a lawyer. I'm tired of this."

"Graves, you want a lawyer?" a Ranger responded, as if he'd caught only a few of my words.

Every time I participated in one of the state's games, I'd come up empty-handed in proving my innocence. "Yeah, I want a lawyer!" I shouted. "Not one of you will believe anything I have to say!"

The Rangers didn't seem to care about my fate, but they did hear me when I spoke this phrase.

"Graves says he wants a lawyer!" one of them yelled.

"Well, all right then," another replied. "Take him back to jail." It was as if I had finally said the magic words, and in legal parlance, that's exactly what I had done. I didn't know it then, but as soon as an accused in a criminal case asks for a lawyer, the police may no longer legally question him or her alone.

It doesn't mean they always follow the rules, but it did ring clear that they all at least *knew* the rules, and I had just invoked the lodestar. I would spend plenty of time while on death row reading about the power of the Sixth Amendment to the Constitution, the one that guarantees the criminally accused the right to be represented at trial. There was a whole lot of "case law" defining what exactly that meant in terms of when my rights were invoked.

Up to that point, I'd believed that the system would sort itself out on my behalf. But it was becoming increasingly obvious that the Rangers weren't interested in the truth. They just wanted to find some way, any way, to get me to say that I was guilty. A confession would be the last nail in my coffin. With that, they would be able to get their conviction and move on.

When it finally dawned on me that the police were trying to build a case against me despite my innocence, I was furious. I thought about my mom and her emotional state. I thought about my children. I was also more determined than ever to prove them wrong. I wasn't about to let them railroad me. I was going to fight for my life.

Growing up in the '70s in Texas exposed young black men like me to casual racism at an early age, and now I had to wonder if I was experiencing the institutional version of it. I remembered being slapped in the face as a kid by my white teacher in the fifth grade because I was laughing at a classmate. Black children knew without being told that white people and authority figures saw us as inferior. I found that not to be universally true when I started having white friends, and my own judgment, but it was a fact of life for nearly everyone in Texas. Generally, up North, you handle race relations differently. You see, you'll pretend whites don't think of blacks as inferior. But they do, just like everywhere else. So you end up keeping it buried under the surface, like a splinter. Now down South, where I'm from, people are more open about their biases. That clear discrimination doesn't feel good, but it does have one advantage. Although we know we'll never be equals in one another's minds, it's the honesty that allows us to be real friends despite the imbalance in our relationships. When it came to the criminal justice system, I believed the system would work for everyone regardless of their race, something I attribute to my government teacher in eighth grade. She taught me to believe that America's criminal justice system was the best in the world. I held on to that belief, and it cost me dearly in these early stages of my case.

The continuing mind games were cruel, but somehow their tactics hardened my resolve. I wasn't going to lie on myself or anyone else, no matter what anyone promised me. I decided then that even if I had to die for the truth, I'd do it. So many people had come before me and pled out to crimes they hadn't committed out of fear in the face of long prison terms, due to lack of resources, and because of a lack of support from family. I didn't care about any of that. I felt determined to stand up for what was right, even if I had to lose my life doing it. I was fired up and ready to take on the criminal justice system, against all the odds. That sense of purpose was invigorating.

I wasn't, at the time, aware of the spiral I had entered. I was "the accused," and this tilt of bias against me would color my every step through the legal system. Starting with my arrest, through an interrogation process engineered to get me to confess, to the lie-detector test I'd been told I'd failed, to the lineup designed to prejudice the viewer against me, it was a downhill slide from the get-go. Multiple studies have shown eyewitness testimony to be the most controversial and flawed of all evidence offered at criminal trials. Now I unfortunately had a much better understanding of why.

So, it was time to get a lawyer.

I racked my brain for a thought on who might help me. My former boss, Roy Allen, was the first name that came to mind. Roy's family owned a machine shop where I'd once worked, and over time he had become a close friend. We started out on the company softball team together; I was at third base and he was the coach. The thought of Roy gave me comfort. I summoned my resolve, understanding that things might finally start going my way if I could get a lawyer. I returned to my cell from the lineup at the Burleson County Courthouse and asked to use the phone, preparing to make a collect call. A jailer passed a bruised, off-white machine into my cell. It had a long extension cord that allowed the jailers to pass it from cell to cell for outgoing calls; no incoming calls were permitted. I dialed the familiar numbers of home, knowing I was costing my family a fortune we didn't have, knowing no one would ever refuse my calls.

"Hey, Mom?"

"Hey!" she exclaimed, happy to hear my voice. "What's up, Son?" I had called my mom every day since my arrest, and she'd always been a champion at lifting my spirits.

"I need you to call Roy Allen," I said. "Tell him to get me a lawyer."

"A lawyer?" My mom couldn't seem to believe what I was saying. She had thought, like me, that this whole ordeal would be resolved within a few days. I could sense the worry in her voice.

"Yeah," I responded. "These damn people don't want the truth. They're playing games." I told her about the lineup.

"They picked you out of a lineup for what?" she asked, obviously confused.

I told her about the gas can and how a woman had claimed she saw me that night.

"How the hell can I be in two places at once?" I asked her. "These folks are full of shit. I want a lawyer."

She assured me that she would call Roy in the morning.

As it turned out, I wasn't the only one with news about the case. "Listen, Son," she said. "The police came down here and took Chee Chee's car somewhere and searched it. They said they were looking for a knife."

I wondered aloud why they would bother my aunt. Investigators had told my mom that they knew I was driving Chee Chee's car. Then it became clear: the affidavit I wrote on Angel's recommendation had come back to bite me. I was relieved, at least, that the prosecutor had actually received what I wrote. My mom and I went back and forth for a minute about the car. It wasn't long before I had to go. Time on the phone was precious, and I wasn't the only inmate at Caldwell that needed to call home.

"I'll call you tomorrow to hear what Roy has to say," I told my mom.

"Keep your head up, Son!" she replied. "Don't you worry. The truth will come out. Just keep saying your prayers." She told me that she loved me. But she couldn't hide her worry.

My cell had never felt colder or emptier. Angel lay on the bottom bunk with a book in his hands, but I was alone in my frustration. My body felt weak. I couldn't eat, and homesickness consumed me. For the first time, I let myself consider that they might keep me there forever.

I had done six months in prison back in 1987 for selling forty dollars' worth of marijuana to an undercover narcotics officer. I'd voluntarily turned myself in to the police after hearing they'd come to my mom's house looking for me. I'd taken responsibility because I'd knowingly put myself in that position. But I also knew I'd never been in that kind of trouble before; I figured I'd get a fine or maybe a few months of probation. Instead, I was overcharged and ended up pleading out to a marijuana *and* cocaine charge to get ten years "shock" probation: 180 days in jail and a criminal record. I was twenty-two then. Of no particular significance to me at the time, the DA on my case was Charles Sebesta. Four years later, this same DA was accusing me of another crime. This time the situation was far different. I was older and more mature. My boys were the focus of my life. The charge was capital murder, which in Texas carries a sentence of death. And I was innocent.

AUGUST 26, 1992:
A FAMILIAR FACE IN COUNTY JAIL

. . . . .

AFTER THE PREVIOUS DAY'S EVENTS, I wasn't interested in breakfast when it came. I had lost a few pounds since my arrest, due to both anxiety and the horrible fare. The food was bland—cold toast and two overcooked eggs. I offered it to Angel.

"Graves, you need to eat something."

"Angel, I'm cool," I assured him. "I just don't have an appetite."

Maybe I would eat at lunch, which at Caldwell consisted of a bologna sandwich and a few chips. I told Angel I was burned out. He nodded in understanding. Somewhere along the line he must have adapted to the jail food. He ate both of our meals.

One of the jailers came soon after with welcome news.

"It's recreation time, gentlemen." It was Steve Jennings, one of the few officers in that place who treated inmates with respect. "Get your clothes on. I'll be back in a few minutes to start pulling you guys out." It was the first such opportunity at Caldwell for a while now. Angel and I rushed to get dressed. We wore jail suits and tennis shoes. A few minutes later, Jennings returned to pull us out. He was workmanlike, clearing cell after cell until each was emptied. Angel and I were the last to go.

The severity of the Texas summer hadn't let up. I stepped outside to waves of September heat that hit my body with force.

There wasn't much to do during recreational time. The rec area consisted of a small patch of half-living grass, nothing like the beautiful baseball field I daydreamed about. Before being framed, I was mostly interested in two things, apart from my sons: baseball and women. I could always close my eyes and disappear into memories of a Texas diamond with perfectly mowed grass and carefully raked dirt, or an old girlfriend who comforted me like heaven and had the soft skin of angels. But that day, the oppressive heat stifled my imagination, and it took all my energy just to focus my eyes around the yard. A surprisingly casual and unimposing chain-link fence encircled the outdoor space, which is why it was hard for Caldwell to organize prison rec time: they first had to find a regular police officer to stand guard on the other side of the fence. Getting an officer to come and stand out there in the Texas weather was a task in and of itself, and it often delayed our emergence into daylight.

Beyond the fence, a car dealership buzzed with people checking out prospective new wheels. Farther down the street was the town square and courthouse where I had testified in front of the grand jury. My eyes wandered north of the jail, to a side street dotted with modest houses. Though it wasn't recreation in the conventional sense, my time outside was cathartic. Like a snowed-in businessman peering at pictures of sunny shores, I feasted on a dream born out of those houses. I knew the stories about the murders were running wild in the local newspapers, but I didn't care about it that much. I longed to be home, my home—back to the familiar places and faces I cared about.

But I was far, far from home now. There was no basketball or handball court in the rec yard, or even a chair to sit on. We had only a blanket and the potential conversation of fellow inmates. It wasn't long before Scotty Burns, my old acquaintance from home, approached me.

"What's up, Anthony?" he asked. "So how do you like this jail?"

I let out a derisive laugh. "Man, this ain't a jail. This is a fucking kennel!"

Scotty laughed in agreement. We exchanged war stories on fighting off the now-notorious mosquitoes. Like the fish in old men's tall tales, the mosquitoes in ours seemed to grow larger with each telling.

Scotty then grew serious. "Man, why did that dude put you in this shit?"

I looked at him with a blank stare. If I hadn't been able to answer that question in my mind after all these weeks, I certainly couldn't explain it to him now.

"I don't know, Scotty," I said. "But this is fucked up." I had welcomed the opportunity to escape those walls just a few minutes before; now, I was back inside.

"When you came in here, they moved everyone around so they could put you in that cell across from Carter," he told me. "I heard y'all talking when you first came in. That's why I hollered at you about the speakers in the cells."

I had told Scotty before that I didn't care about the speakers, and my answer remained the same. I just wanted everybody to hear the truth.

"Scotty, why you in here anyway, man?"

"Aw, man! I had a shootout with some dudes, and now they're trying to give me an attempted murder case!" Scotty had been involved in a shooting near College Station. He told me that they'd had him in Caldwell awaiting trial for almost a year. I wondered if it might be that long before I saw a trial. Surrounded by guys with dire legal problems, I heard about many struggles with the system, but rarely did I consider the *duration* of their battles. I had spent my first weeks in jail believing my innocence would save me, but now I had to seriously start to question *when*.

My inability to answer Scotty's question gnawed at me. I just knew there had to be some procedure in place to protect a person from being arrested on the strength of a single lie. I also wondered about Carter and what had been going on in his head. Of all the people in the world, why did he choose me?

"I even have alibi witnesses," I told Scotty. "People who know good and well where I was."

"You know these Rangers been asking me questions about you," he said. "They pulled a bunch of us out and asked if you and Carter talked about anything."

I was confused and angered by this, though not surprised. I hadn't said much to Carter, and Scotty had told the police as much.

An hour later, we were herded back into our cells. I lay flat on my bunk, thinking about what Scotty had said.

"Say, Angel, Scotty told me that the Rangers were pulling people out to see if they heard Carter and me talking about anything," I told him.

"Yeah, man, these damn laws are trying to get anything on you," he advised. "So be careful in here."

What Angel didn't say was as important as what he had said. He didn't mention being pulled out himself, yet he somehow knew that it had been going on. The thought of Angel being a plant to extract information from me was too much. Maybe they just hadn't gotten around to pulling him yet, I reasoned. Looking back, this thought was foolish. Angel had been my cellmate, certainly the person in closest proximity to me and probably the one I felt most comfortable around. Angel would have been the first to field questions. I tried to quiet my mind, but falling asleep in jail was hard. Aside from the bugs that scarcely took a night off, the heat caused my body to stick to the cell's poor excuse for a mattress. My mind raced with thoughts about my case. My body felt at once restless and exhausted. Too often, my arms and legs failed to sync up with my brain. It was only after hours of struggle that I fell asleep that night.

Two days later, the jailer was at our cell.

"Get dressed, Angel," he said. "I'm taking you over to the house." Someone wanted to talk to him. I tried not to make too much of it. After all, officers had talked to plenty of people. When Angel returned, though, his expression gave me some pause.

"Angel, is everything OK?" I pressed.

"Man, those were the Texas Rangers out there. They called me over and started asking me lots of questions about you. I told them you hadn't told me anything and that I don't know anything." The Rangers had asked Angel whether he believed that I had killed the family in Somerville.

This would be something to discuss with my lawyer, if I ever got one. I was talking with Mom every day about it, and I knew Roy would come through, but in the meantime I had to sit and wait for it to actually happen.

"I told them that you said you didn't do it and that I believe you," Angel said, his words less than reassuring in that moment. "I don't want anything to do with this shit. I've got enough problems of my own."

Something in Angel had changed. The easy comfort with which we'd initially conversed had disappeared. Maybe he was starting to feel the pressure from his own situation, as DA Sebesta appeared to be moving his prosecution forward. Angel now wanted to know more about my case, and as a result, the cell felt small.

"What exactly happened to those people?" he asked. He demanded details on how and why they were killed. I remembered from our early conversations that Angel already knew all about the crime. He knew the particulars of how the children had been stabbed, how their bodies were doused with gasoline.

"Carter doesn't know me, Angel," I told him, trying to set him at ease. "All I know is that he's married to a cousin of mine." I explained again, for what seemed like the hundredth time, that Robert Carter couldn't provide even the simplest details about my life, like where I lived or what they called me on the streets.

Angel only nodded impassively, as if my answer wasn't what he wanted to hear.

The Rangers weren't done pulling inmates from their cells. Later that night, they had conversations with several more men. They'd held me for a couple of weeks now without credible evidence, and they needed something to keep the game going. I was worried. Robert Carter had lied on me for what seemed like no reason at all. What was going to stop someone else from doing the same? I had come to Caldwell with trust in the system and in my fellow man. By that night, the days of looking over my shoulder had gotten the best of me. I was suspicious of everyone, doubtful whether there was anyone in Burleson County I could trust.

SEPTEMBER-OCTOBER 1992:
BOND HEARING, INDICTMENT, AND GOING TO COURT WITH DICK DEGUERIN, THE MOST RESPECTED ATTORNEY IN ALL OF TEXAS

· · · · ·

THE NEXT MORNING BROUGHT with it all the familiar noises in the jail where I now spent all my time. Inmates began their usual routine of out-talking one another. A trusty brought food and other items from door to door. I sat up in my bed, relieved to part from the mattress I'd fought through most of the night. A jailer approached my cell with news.

"Graves, you've got an attorney visit," he told me.

My heart leapt. It seemed the first truly good news I'd received in the short but awful time since my arrest and replenished my reserves with remarkable speed. I hopped down from the bunk and dressed quickly. The jailer took me to a small room out front, sparsely furnished with a table and a couple of chairs.

A short man who looked to be in his fifties sat before me. He had a composed demeanor, as if he had sat in that same room waiting to speak to an accused murderer many times before. One leg was crossed over the other at the knee, a well-polished black dress boot dangling in controlled suspension.

"Anthony?" he asked. "My name is Dick DeGuerin. I've been hired by a friend of yours to represent you."

"How are you?" I asked, unsure how to begin.

"I'm doing fine, Anthony," he said. "The better question is, how are you doing?"

"To be honest, I'm not too good," I told him. "I'm sitting in a jail for a crime I don't know anything about."

"That's the reason I'm here, Anthony." He struck me as sincere. By that point, I'd encountered enough people who didn't believe in my innocence that I was able to spot one who did. He was also prepared, with papers and what seemed like a plan. As we reviewed my case, his questions were precise, eliciting from me answers that seemed to build a narrative. I was far from an expert on defense lawyers, but our conversation told me he knew his way around the court system. He confirmed my thoughts on the case as our time came to a close.

"Son, they don't have anything on you. I want to ask them about this polygraph test that you took because they don't have anything about it in their files." I nodded as he spoke. He was in the zone, learning and uncovering what I thought were the oddest parts of the state's investigations. I didn't want to disrupt his flow.

"I'll get back with you next week," he said. "We can go over a few more details then." He gave me his card and an open invitation to call if I had any problems. I wondered to myself what he might be able to do about the mosquitoes.

DeGuerin left me with one bit of parting advice.

"Make sure you don't speak to anyone about the case because these damn Rangers play by their own rules. They'll probably have someone in this jail to try to get you to tell them something." Indeed, they already had.

I didn't know at the time that Dick DeGuerin was one of the most respected attorneys in all of Texas. He would go on to represent several high-profile clients, winning dismissals and acquittals at startling rates. I just knew that he believed in me, and in one sentence he had perfectly described the little game the Rangers were playing with me. I saw for the first time how all the things that didn't seem quite right were really a part of the state's attempt to make a case out of thin air.

I returned to my cell on a wave of optimism.

"Say, Angel! I got a lawyer and he seems good. Dick DeGuerin's his name."

"What?" Angel said, unable to conceal his surprise. "He's one of the best in Texas, maybe even the world. You'll be well represented."

I needed to call my mom. A jailer passed me the familiar phone through my cell door. It rang just once before she picked up.

"Momma, you must have gotten in touch with Roy Allen. My attorney came up here to see me today."

She told me that she had talked to Roy and that he'd assured her that he would find a good attorney.

"Give him the news and tell him thanks," I said. "From what I can tell, it seems like he picked a good one." It had been a while since I had good news to report. Mom could hardly contain her excitement. Her mood eased, and she had stories to tell about my kids and the family. She would always make sure to tell me about my sons, like when she had last seen them or talked to them.

Momma also kept me up on what my brothers and sisters were doing, how shocked everyone was about my situation, and how supportive they all were. I appreciated her words, but they made me miss home all the more.

Dick DeGuerin made good on his promise to visit me a week later. We met in that same front room and Dick got straight to the point.

"Anthony, I want you to know that I've filed a motion for a speedy hearing. We need to find out what they think they have on you." His tone was reassuring. I had gathered during these first weeks in Caldwell that the state was stalling, putting me in a position to fail.

"I don't think they have shit," he continued. "We're going to push them to take us to trial." He radiated confidence. I would come to learn that he was not only known for winning at trial, but for using his reputation for aggressiveness as leverage against the state in pretrial proceedings. I sat quietly as he outlined his strategy.

"I've talked to the prosecutor about the results of the polygraph test you took down in Houston. He claims he doesn't know anything about it. Did you know they gave one to Carter too?"

"No, I didn't," I told him.

"Well, Carter failed his. They have the results of his test. Somehow, they don't have the results of yours. Sebesta maintains that he didn't even know you had taken it."

I was stunned.

"Look, Anthony, I know they're full of shit," he said. "Do you remember who the polygraph operator was?" I filed through my thoughts and remembered the big black man who had administered the test. I remembered how he'd sat where I couldn't see his expression and how I'd heard him tearing small bits of paper while the machine did its business. I mentioned the name of the person I thought it was.

"Yeah, I know him," Dick responded. The look in his eyes told me that he didn't think too highly of the ranger, to say the least.

Dick was insistent. It might have taken me a few weeks to piece it all together, but he didn't share my naïveté. Whatever ideals I'd associated with the American justice system as being the best in the world, Dick had seen enough of the system to know its warts. He sniffed out bullshit like one of the hounds the jailers used to track down escaped inmates.

The Rangers had taken my clothes the day I was arrested. After hearing what Dick had said about the missing polygraph results, I had a sneaking suspicion my clothes had gone missing as well. I explained to Dick that on the day of my arrest, the Rangers had wanted to conduct some analysis on what I was wearing. I'd given them everything they asked for, right down to my tennis shoes. Dick hadn't seen them. He'd explored my case file and had no knowledge of any such tests. He assured me that he would look into it.

In jail, the days passed slowly. I read books that I pulled out of the jail library, mostly westerns and also the Bible. No one was able to send me any type of reading material at that point, so I just read what I could get my hands on. I had not been a reader back home, so this new habit, born of necessity, took some time to develop. But once it did, I read voraciously and discovered a new part of myself that loved books.

When I wasn't reading, my days in jail were consumed by the occasional visit to the rec yard and conversations with fellow inmates. The conversation was mostly about sports, women, money, and street life.

Before being locked up, my days had been filled with just living life the best I understood it at the time. Sometimes clumsily, other times with not enough purpose, but always with an understanding that if I stayed out of trouble, life would be good to me in return. And it had: I worked, played sports, spent time with family, flirted with women, and tried to find myself and a place in the world that felt right for me. I didn't live a big life. But now, I missed everything about it.

In jail, I had almost zero freedom to decide anything for myself. It was no longer up to me when I could shower, go outside, take a walk, turn the lights on or off, visit friends, go to the store, change jobs, choose my own meals, or enjoy any other basic freedom that comes with being alive in

America. They took everything but what I held inside—the part of me that I now protected like a priceless jewel, because if this was stolen too, the way I saw it, the State of Texas might as well kill me now.

Reduced to that, I mostly thought about my case day after day, even though there wasn't much I could do about it. I'd been in jail for close to a month and I hadn't even been arraigned at a bond hearing yet. A couple more weeks passed before that happened, finally, on October 7.

That morning, Dick came to the jail prior to the courtroom proceeding.

"I need to prepare you for what might happen, Anthony. Don't expect to get a bond today."

"Why is that?" I asked. In our last meeting, Dick had exposed holes in the state's case. I was concerned by his change of tone. Dick was pragmatic, though, seeing all the angles. He knew enough to know that the law wasn't all that mattered.

"Well, it's an election year, Anthony. There's no way the judge will take a chance on letting you make bond, in case the papers make a big deal out of it."

Dick was right. The worst thing a newspaper can print about a judge is a headline proclaiming "Suspected Killer Out of Jail." Of course, he had a plan. He explained that we might get bond by moving my case to another court. I was happy to have him on my side.

My mother had brought a dark suit to jail for me to wear during my court appearance. It fit a little looser, no doubt a consequence of my lack of appetite for what passed as food at Caldwell. I looped a tie into a double Windsor and pulled the knot tight to the button on my neck. It felt good to be out of the orange jumpsuit.

As I entered the courtroom, I immediately spotted my mother, other members of my family, and Yolanda, whom I hadn't seen since the morning after the murders. They sat on wooden benches in the back of the room. Yolanda shared my mother's tense expression. This was all so nerve-wracking for me, and I knew it had to be just as hard on my loved ones, who had even less information than the scraps I was given to help them process this nightmare. While we had shared plenty of phone calls early on in my incarceration, this was my first time actually seeing her since my arrest, and that was emotional for me, not only because of my feelings for her but because she was the one person in the world who'd known exactly where I was the entire night of the murders. She'd been in bed beside me. It hadn't taken long for our communication to dry up after my arrest, though, as her father had put an end to our calls after receiving a $3,000 phone bill, and she was moving on with her life, anyway. That day everyone was there in court for me, though, and I was happy to see them.

District Attorney Sebesta and four Texas Rangers were there, too, indicating the level of gravity the state was placing on my case. A conviction and a closed murder case sure went a lot further for the DA and the Rangers than an unsolved multiple homicide on the books. But somehow none of them seemed as imposing with Dick DeGuerin in the room. I took my place next to Dick as the judge made his entrance. We stood for the standard ceremony before a bailiff told us to sit. I couldn't help feeling like I was on a television show.

The judge was quick to cut the silence. "Counsel, do either of you wish to file any pending or additional matters with this court prior to proceeding?" Both Dick and Sebesta said no. We were ready to go.

The hearing began with Sebesta calling his first witness. It was the fire marshal who had been assigned to the crime scene on the night of the murders. He described in gruesome detail the situation he'd encountered at the house. He gave an important expert opinion—that the fire was started by gasoline. The marshal remembered with remarkable clarity the location of each body. Sebesta seemed to know just what to ask to elicit the most emotional response from his witness. He had the marshal recall the stab wounds and gunshot holes that riddled the victims' bodies. The testimony was gut-wrenching and brutal.

Before long, it was time for Dick's turn. His questions on cross-examination were simple and purposeful. He knew that certain facts were needed for the record.

"Did you find any signs of forced entry?" he asked.

"No, I didn't," the marshal responded.

My lawyer followed up with a series of other questions.

Sebesta's next witness was Shawn Eldridge. I recognized him as the Caldwell jailer who had booked me when I first arrived and one of the many uniformed officials who had hovered around my case in those first few days. Describing the booking process, Eldridge testified that he'd kept the speaker on in my cell and that he'd heard me talking to Robert Carter. His hand having just been on the Bible, Eldridge looked straight ahead with piercing eyes as he insisted that I'd made incriminating comments in those conversations. Sebesta seemed satisfied, having picked up something useful against me. Dick, though, had little trouble ripping gaping holes in the jailer's testimony. A once-confident Eldridge became reluctant. His testimony on cross-examination revealed commonsense deficiencies in his narrative. Eldridge hadn't discussed my statements with anyone for three weeks, an unlikely twist considering the importance of that evidence. He made no notes about what he'd heard and only "remembered" it after a conversation with the Rangers.

"Why would you wait three weeks to tell anyone something so important?" Dick pressed, his question saying as much as any answer could. Eldridge was dumbstruck. He was then asked about the notoriously unreliable speakers in the Caldwell facility. He acknowledged that the speakers were erratic, sometimes working and other times not, and admitted that the speakers were even known to display the wrong cell number. What started as a boxing match between Dick and the jailer had turned into something else. Eldridge was helpless, curled tightly against the ropes, taking punch after withering punch. I focused only on the reddening of the jailer's face. His lies exposed, Eldridge scurried off the stand.

Knowing Eldridge's testimony was weak, Sebesta next called to the stand another jailer, to try again. This jailer testified that he, too, heard me talking to Carter about what I'd done on that August night. His story seemed to have been elicited to address the problems uncovered by Dick in the Eldridge exchange. The jailer had taken measures to record the conversation, or so he said. He testified that he had gone to his car to retrieve a tape recorder. The recorder had conveniently failed to function properly. Dick wasn't any kinder to this witness.

"Officer, did you see Anthony Graves on the night he was booked in?"

"No, I didn't." The officer fidgeted in his seat. He hadn't seen Officer Eldridge collapse under pressure, but he surely felt the force of my lawyer's heavy-handed questions.

"I see," Dick continued. "Have you ever heard Anthony Graves's voice?"

The jailer said that he hadn't. Dick then asked whether this jailer had thought to report what he had heard. The jailer said that he'd kept the information to himself, a claim that sounded as unlikely the second time as it had the first.

Dick pressed the jailer on the proper procedure for prison personnel. Weren't they supposed to report such vital information as soon as they got it? The jailer was visibly shaken. He looked like he would rather be anywhere else in the world. This urge was confirmed when Dick finally let him off the stand.

"No further questions," Dick said, turning away from the witness stand. The jailer moved quickly out of the courtroom.

Watching him leave the stand, I felt a swell of satisfaction. It was a brief moment of respite. I was there under the protection of a good attorney, and the jailers who had tried so hard to make my life hell were now under pressure. Between watching Eldridge slither off the stand and feeling the obvious discomfort of a second shamed officer, I indulged a bit in the raging resentment that had been building since the moment my mother's neighbor told me the cops were on my trail. I wasn't exactly comfortable with how I felt in that moment. Mostly it was a small burst of power and control to break up the monotony of jail-induced helplessness.

The seemingly endless parade of witnesses continued with Ranger Ray Coffman, the lead investigator on my case. Not much had changed in Coffman's dress or demeanor since he took control of my first interrogation. He still had that same walk that made me chuckle to myself. He walked with an air of importance. He had on his big white cowboy hat with a pair of boots that seemed too tight for him to walk in. He was a clown to me, but his work on my case was not funny. He still moved slowly, too, as if in defiance of anyone who might deign to tell him what to do. He wore sunglasses this time, refusing to take them off when he walked into the room. His smooth, unhurried responses confirmed that his confidence wasn't an act. He clearly described what he'd observed at the crime scene. He outlined the contours of his hours-long conversation with Robert Carter. Dick knew that unlike the two jailers who had testified before, Coffman was a strong witness. His testimony was likely to resonate not only with the judge but with a jury, if we ever got to trial.

The contrast between Ranger Coffman and my attorney was stark. Dick was short. His suit looked as if it'd been tailor-made for him. He was intellectual, with a mind that moved from point A to point C before most people had passed B. He had an understated competence. Dick knew what he was doing and didn't need to do much more than open his mouth to prove it. Coffman was different. He wore his boots and sunglasses like a shield, broadcasting to the world that he was somebody important. Their matchup looked, on the surface, like a heavyweight tilt between comparably formidable foes. And maybe it would have been, had they met on the street or in some dusty barroom. But this was a courtroom, and few in Texas commanded a courtroom like Dick DeGuerin.

Dick kept his questions simple, but he was still able to shake Coffman's confidence. The Ranger's once-brazen demeanor wilted in a matter of seconds as he struggled to answer questions. He looked nervous, almost confused. I thought for a minute that he might pull out a cigarette and chain-puff it right there on the witness stand. That thought almost made me smile. Dick scored a blow with a question that caught Coffman flat-footed.

"Mr. Coffman, is there anything you have, or have discovered during your investigation, that would link my client, Anthony Graves, to this case?"

"No, sir," he said. "There is nothing that I have that would link your client to this case." His comment struck me as the sort of thing you might hear at an exoneration hearing. The lead investigator had admitted under oath that he'd found no evidence to link me to the murders. That led to a more disturbing thought. Why, in light of all that had just been said, did these people still want me so badly?

Dick responded to Coffman's comments by seizing momentum. The hearing was to determine whether or not I'd be granted bail, and Dick thought the Ranger's admission was more than enough for the judge to set a reasonable amount. I was excited, thinking about the possibilities. But the judge denied his request. I added that moment to the growing catalogue of inexplicable denials. Many times the Rangers, jailers, police, and now the courts had refused to grant my freedom despite clear indications of innocence. It dawned on me that the state might just be capable of anything.

Since this was a bond hearing, the only issue was whether a bond would be ordered by the court and thus grant me a path to fight while free (assuming I could somehow afford to pay the bond), or whether I would be remanded, meaning held without bond. In bond hearings, there really isn't much reason for the defense to present evidence. In fact, the entire burden of proof is on the prosecutor, at this hearing and at all stages of the proceedings. The DA wanted me remanded, of course, but at the same time didn't want to show his hand in advance of trial. So the prosecution offered the least evidence it could that would result in an outcome of remand.

It's also not for the defense to present its case right then, as it would have little or no impact on the bond decision, and it would tip off the prosecutor to the defense's strategy, thus helping them better prepare. By that point everyone knew my alibi; it would not be news here. So, strategically, Dick did not put up much of a defense.

As expected, I was remanded. Dick knew all this too well; it was me who was learning about something I never wanted to know, particularly when I was sitting in the defendant's chair. I wouldn't be going anywhere in a capital case unless or until this nightmare somehow ended through the legal process.

Back in my cell, I lay in my bunk thinking about the day's events. I thought of my family, their reactions in the courtroom. Like me, they were beginning to understand how unjust every aspect of my case was. And I wasn't surprised by the judge's ruling, because Dick had already told me what he would do. Still, I was disappointed to see this man—who'd been elected judge—seemingly allow politics to play a role in dispensing justice.

It all felt like a whirlwind of good and bad. I'd been elated during the trial as the Rangers and the police department were exposed as a cabal of liars, but the denial of bail tempered my emotions.

I called my mom to talk about what had happened in the hearing. We shared a laugh, a perverse commiseration on a case that tended more to politics than to truth. While we both knew my calls were too expensive for her to receive this often, a mother's grace and love kept her from ever mentioning that burden, not even once.

. . . . .

Movement in my case seemed to come in three-week increments. I waited as patiently as I could to learn what would come next.

One night I stood at my cell door about a week after my court date, trying to catch a bit of television through the crack. Officer Eldridge approached my cell. He held in his hand a bundle of legal papers.

"What's this?" I asked him.

"They're indictment papers, Graves. You've been indicted." My heart plummeted. All those weeks in jail had cultivated an alarm within me, which buzzed uncontrollably whenever it sensed bullshit, as it did in that moment.

"Man! I don't want this! I need a phone so I can call my attorney. How the fuck are they going to indict me for something I didn't do? I want to call my attorney!"

"Graves, it's after nine. You can use the phone in the morning."

I didn't care. The word "indictment" had hit me so hard that I knew I'd never sleep without some assurance from my lawyer. Eldridge finally relented and brought the phone. I soon had Dick DeGuerin on the line.

"Dick! This is Anthony Graves," I said. "The jailer just brought me some indictment papers." I was indignant, but careful not to take out my frustration on him.

"I'm not surprised. If the DA wants an indictment, he usually gets it. It doesn't mean anything other than the fact that they plan to take us to court. I'll check on it in the morning and get back with you."

"Look, man, I just want to go home," I told him. "I'm tired of their games."

Dick assured me that everything would be all right. He then turned the conversation in a different direction.

"Say, Anthony, have you heard from Roy Allen at all?"

"No, I haven't."

"Well, I've been trying to reach him to get the rest of the payment for taking on your case. I'm having difficulty getting together with him."

I assured him that Roy Allen was good for the money. Dick seemed satisfied with my answer, but I was worried. Lawyers of DeGuerin's stature take payment at two points. They charge a fee to investigate the case and handle pretrial motions, as Dick had done. A much larger payment is required to take the case to trial. I didn't know exactly how much Dick DeGuerin charged, but something told me he wouldn't be having that conversation with me unless there was some doubt about Roy Allen's ability to pay.

LATE OCTOBER 1992–MAY 1993:
THE WAITING GAME

· · · · ·

CELL ASSIGNMENTS WERE FLUID IN CALDWELL. Not long after I talked to Dick, the jailers moved me from the cell I'd shared with Angel and placed me with a familiar face: Scotty. The move was a welcome one. Scotty was the only person in Caldwell who I was acquainted with from home. I trusted him as much as I could trust anyone in the Burleson County facility. Though welcome, the move was also curious. I had been in a two-man cell with Angel. Scotty's cell had only one bunk. One of us would be sleeping on the floor, and I was pretty sure it wouldn't be him. I moved quickly past my confusion. It wasn't worth thinking about, with the many other things clouding my mind. And I didn't mind sleeping on the floor, reasoning that I'd easily trade that inconvenience for a cellmate I thought I could trust. Besides, the beds weren't all that comfortable anyway.

My conversations with Scotty during those first few days were easy. We talked about the places we'd been and the people we had known. Though he and I hadn't been good friends back in Brenham, I grew up with one of his cousins, so I had seen him around. Talking with him was the closest I got to normal while at Caldwell. The jailers must have sensed our comfort. After only a couple of days, the Rangers came calling.

"Scotty?" one of them asked. "We want to talk to you." I watched as they pulled Scotty from the cell, just as they'd done with Angel and others before. I shook my head. It wasn't hard to see that something was wrong when Scotty returned.

"Man, Graves!" he said, his voice shaking. "They just started coming at me with questions about you, rapid-fire style. There wasn't anything to say. I know nothin' about nothin'!"

I was overwhelmed. I racked my brain for a good reason they were hounding me. I couldn't say much to Scotty in the moments that followed. I needed my mom. After some wrangling, the jailer brought me a phone, and I dialed home, collect as always. I asked her about my children and how she was doing. I wanted to know about my brothers and sisters too. Just a few weeks before, I had been like a dad to them. Our own father had left when we were young, leaving my mother to raise us around her work schedule. I wondered how my family was doing without me.

Scotty asked to take a turn on the line with my mom, and I said sure. He reported what had happened with the Rangers and told her that Sebesta, too, had talked to him about my case. Sebesta was dealing, giving Scotty a chance at reduced time if he'd give the state something to work with. I don't expect Sebesta much cared whether the information was true or not; it needed only to be useful. The thought of Scotty lying on me kept me up at night. I trusted Scotty and all, but I was quickly learning the pressures that confinement could put on a man.

· · · · ·

Pretrial detention is largely a waiting game. A man sent to the penitentiary with a sentence can set his mind to doing whatever time he's assigned. A man in my position had no such luxury. I waited as weeks turned into months.

I was starting to feel sorry for myself. I couldn't help but wonder, *Why me?* Why would God put me through this if He's real? I'm a good guy. I'd never had any malice in my heart. Why would Robert Carter get me caught up in all this?

I was terribly homesick and missed my sons. One night I took up the Bible and hurled it into a corner. I wanted to give up. I wasn't sleeping well. I finally realized I wasn't going home anytime soon. I cried. I wept. I was afraid.

Then I walked over to the corner of the cell and picked the Good Book back up. It opened to a passage that told me God wouldn't put any more on me than I could bear.

> There has no temptation taken you but such as is common to man: but God is faithful, who will not suffer you to be tempted above that you are able; but will with the temptation also make a way to escape, that you may be able to bear it. (1 Corinthians 10: 13)

It was a rough night.

I knew that something would happen in my case eventually, but the timing was out of my control. Often, the waiting was interrupted only by happenstance, when conversations with jailers would give me insights into my own case. Such was the case when Officer Jennings came through to check the row. He moved from cell to cell, passing the phone with each stop. Finally, he was at my door.

"Hey Graves, how are you doing?"

"Not too good, Steve," I told him. "The grand jury handed down an indictment."

Jennings nodded. "I heard about that. But hey, don't be pissed off at the sheriff. He didn't want you in this jail. He thought they didn't have any evidence to be bringing you here." He said this almost as if he was trying to offload some guilt.

"The sheriff told us all that if the media asks about your case, we're to tell them that it's still under investigation," he continued.

I knew it had been reported in the media that two suspects had been charged with the crime in the Somerville murders. Jennings went on to describe the way that Sebesta had gone over the sheriff's head and brought in the Texas Rangers. They were the ones who'd put me in jail, not the folks from county. Up until that point, I hadn't made much of a distinction between the different law enforcement agencies. The Rangers had played head games, local lawman Lou Larson had tried to intimidate me, and even the jailers had made things up at the bail hearing. But it seemed clear in that moment that the Rangers were driving all of it. Jennings left me with a word of encouragement: all twelve jurors would need to find me guilty if they were going to lock me away.

Among the many practical problems that jail poses for inmates is the fact that you can do hardly anything useful with the information you get. When jailers passed on relevant nuggets or fellow inmates gave me insight on the state's tactics, all I could do was wait for the next visit from my lawyer to try to make sense of what I'd heard. It was a couple of weeks before Dick DeGuerin was back at Caldwell to check in on me. We met in the same small office that had become our de facto war room.

Dick started the conversation as he always did. "How are you doing, Anthony?"

"I'm not so good, sir," I replied. "I'm tired of being in here."

"Well, I'll tell you this. I checked on the indictment, and they plan on taking you to trial on this case."

Frustration once again began to rise in me. "But how in the hell can they do that for something I didn't do?" How many times had I asked this question? That's the problem with simple questions that go unanswered. I figured I would just keep on asking until someone explained.

"Sebesta's a chickenshit son of a bitch, Anthony. He would try to convict a ham sandwich. Don't you worry. I'll prove your innocence." I had already heard that damn ham sandwich metaphor and it was starting to irritate me.

But I believed Dick DeGuerin. I was having a hard time proving my own innocence, especially knowing I shouldn't have had to. If anyone in Texas could make the state see the light, it was my diminutive yet powerful attorney.

"I need to talk to you about Roy Allen," Dick said, shifting gears away from the particulars of my case. His tone made me suddenly uneasy. "It seems he's having trouble getting the rest of the money together. Anthony, I can't do my job effectively without the money that's necessary for this kind of case. If he can't get the money to me, the only thing I can do is to ask the judge to appoint me to your case as assigned counsel."

"I'm sure that Roy Allen will get the money to you, sir."

"Well, I'll give him another call and see what he's come up with."

I knew that trying a capital case can cost thousands of dollars in experts and investigators alone. Not even counting what Dick would expect for his time, the costs for a case like mine could stretch into the six-figure range. I didn't want to think about the fact that the question of my freedom might come down to whether my people could raise the requisite cash.

After our meeting, I called Momma to let her know about the financial tension with Dick. "He says that Roy Allen is having trouble with the money," I explained.

"What does he mean by 'having trouble'?"

"The worst kind. Apparently Roy hasn't been able to come up with it all."

"Well, how much is he supposed to pay?" she asked.

I didn't know how to answer her. Sure, I knew Dick's reputation as a trial lawyer. I'd seen his expensive shoes and suits. But I only had my jailhouse counselors (my fellow inmates) to get me in the ballpark of what a high-profile attorney like Dick DeGuerin charged his clients.

"I think it's about $150,000," I finally conceded. That seemed an impossibly large sum, even for someone like Roy Allen. My mom was shocked. She had spoken with Dick a few days earlier and he'd assured her that he had everything he needed to get me out of jail. She said she would get in touch with Roy and asked that I call her back in an hour.

I was anxious as I waited. It wasn't much more than goodwill that had prompted Roy Allen to bankroll my legal defense fund. And $150,000 was a *lot* of goodwill.

As soon as I could secure phone access again, I made the call, my anxiety mounting with each ring. When my mom finally answered, she sounded dejected as she told me about her conversation with Roy.

"Son," she said, "he seems to think it's a lot of money, and he feels Dick is sandbagging on your case to get even more."

I started to read between the lines. "What does that mean?" I asked, not sure I wanted to know.

"Roy says he doesn't have that kind of money. He's asked his brothers to help him, but I guess they didn't give him anything. The long and the short of it is that he's not going to pay Dick to defend you."

We were both silent as the implications of this statement hit home. "This is messed up, Momma!" I said, doing a bad job of concealing my panic. "He has the money." It was true. Roy did have the money. He just wasn't going to spend it on this. I was a groomsman at his wedding and a close personal confidant, but friendships have limits, especially when it comes to money, and I had found the edge of mine with Roy. I didn't blame him; it was a huge ask. Still, I was at the end of my rope. Dick DeGuerin was my key to getting out of this mess.

"Anthony, you just got to keep up the faith," my mother said, as if reading my thoughts. "Everything is going to work out. Don't let these damn folks upset you like this."

"Momma, doesn't anybody understand?" I asked. "I'm the one living in this piece of shit. Every day I have to look at the messed-up food. And worse, they're dragging my name through the fucking mud." I apologized for my language. I was hot, and frustrated, and tired of hitting my head against a wall.

Mom promised to call Roy Allen again, and she assured me that if he didn't pay the legal fees, she'd quit her job—at the time she was a dorm supervisor for the Brenham State School—and cash in on her savings. She had around $20,000 in her retirement account, an amount she'd worked her entire life to save.

"I don't want you to do that, Momma," I started to say, but she cut me off.

"I think I can get my job back after I've been gone for six months," she said. "Don't worry about a thing, all right? Just keep your head up and pray to God."

Prison life was slow. There was plenty of time to talk to God. Most guys took the opportunity, and most got no direct relief.

"Yeah, well, I've been praying. And I'm still here."

"Anthony," she said, her voice filled with sudden resolve. "Pray some more."

. . . . .

My mom's conversation with Roy Allen the next day changed nothing: it was clear he wasn't going to cover Dick DeGuerin's fees. He had talked about finding another attorney to represent me, but I had lost hope that Roy was going to come through with the help I needed. I tried to understand. I knew it was a lot of money. Maybe he had lost confidence in me, or in my innocence. But I was beginning to despair. It felt like a cruel joke. Dick had told me that he'd ask to be appointed to the case by the court. But I didn't expect this would happen, as he was well beyond the price range of court-assigned counsel. And I really didn't think he would take my case at a steep discount, not with all the demand for his services. It wasn't long before a letter addressed to me put an end to my wondering.

Dear Mr. Graves,

I have informed the Judge that I will be taking myself off of your case. It seems that your friend does not have the money to retain my services, and I can no longer represent you.

I want you to know that I believe in your innocence and I wish you the best of luck.

Dick DeGuerin
January 1993

Just like that, one of the country's best defense lawyers slipped through my hands, despite his stated belief in my innocence. His well-wishes didn't do much to ease the pain. Dick had understood perfectly the game the state had been playing in my case. But still he walked away.

Meanwhile, my mom had been working on a backup plan. She told me that my brother's girlfriend worked for an attorney in Bellville named Calvin Garvie. He had heard about my case and expressed an interest in representing me. I was relieved but unsure. I knew by this point that I needed help in navigating the uncertain waters of the Texas legal system. But I knew nothing about Calvin Garvie or his ability to guide me.

After reaching out to Mr. Garvie to talk with him about his price for handling my case, my mom arranged for him to meet with me the following week.

In May 1993, the attorney came up to the old Caldwell jail to pay me a visit. The officer escorted me into the small attorney-client room inside the jail where I could visit privately with him, just as I had with Dick. A short, bald black man with a round face and glasses, Calvin struck me as a bit of a nerd. He had a habit, as he talked, of putting his finger up to his glasses to push them further up his nose. I immediately felt comfortable with him.

He might have been forty years old, not much younger than Dick DeGuerin. But Dick had been experienced in cases like mine; Calvin was green.

Calvin must have sensed my uneasiness. He talked for a minute about his experience. He had handled many cases over the course of his career, but only one of them had been for capital murder. Even then, the case had ended in a plea bargain long before the client's life hung in the balance.

Despite his lack of experience, I liked Calvin. He spoke softly, his voice a welcome change from the shouting that surrounded me in my cell. Like Dick, he saw right through the holes in the state's case. I was drawn in as he described what he considered the state's fabrications in their case against me. His familiarity with the details of the case was reassuring. He was from close to home, I learned, and he knew some of my people, so he'd been following my predicament from the start. My mom felt comfortable with him too. Calvin Garvie wasn't Dick DeGuerin, but by the time he left the jail that day, he'd become my new attorney.

Calvin informed me that he wouldn't be working the case by himself. It's typical for attorneys to work in teams on capital cases: the time simply spent investigating a case is difficult for one person. Lydia Clay-Jackson would be sitting second-chair. I didn't have much to go on in evaluating whether they were up to the task. Dick DeGuerin had a reputation that preceded him. Calvin Garvie did not. Then again, I was innocent, and how hard can it be to represent an innocent man?

My mom quit the job that she'd had for more than nineteen years to cash in her retirement annuity. She gave Calvin Garvie $10,000 up front and shelled out another grand for an investigator.

PART TWO

TRIAL, CONVICTION, AND SENTENCING

*If the system turns away from the abuses inflicted on the guilty,
then who can be next but the innocents?*

—MICHAEL CONNELLY,
The Concrete Blonde

SEPTEMBER 1993:
A YEAR SINCE ARREST

· · · · ·

NOT ALL PRISONS ARE CREATED EQUAL. While they all constrain an individual's freedom, some make everyday life a bit more intolerable for inmates than others. The Caldwell jail was among the worst. By September 1993, my case was at a standstill. By this time I had been in jail a little over a year, long enough to experience the county's breaking in of a new facility. On the instructions of the jailers, I packed my few belongings and waited. The transport process was far from simple. It felt like the old Texas football games, where every cop in town was on hand to help. Officers played an elaborate game of fetch, moving inmates from their cells to cars, then coming back for more. I grew increasingly impatient, watching as officers repeatedly bypassed my cell in favor of moving other inmates.

"Hey!" I called out to Officer Steve Jennings, the one jailer who'd been kind to me during my time there. "What's going on? I'm ready to go!"

Steve informed me they were plucking me last, without offering an explanation. As the transfer process continued to play out, my impatience soon turned to boredom. Finally, Officer Larson approached my cell. It had been more than a year since we'd shared a high-speed ride to and from the suspect polygraph test on the night of my arrest. I had a pretty good idea of how this would go. I had watched for hours as inmates before me had been moved without incident. I had a feeling things wouldn't go so smoothly with Larson. On his demand, I slid my hands through the pan hole of my cell door. He slapped the handcuffs on a few clicks too tight, as was his custom. Not content to stop with my hands, Larson made me get down on my knees so he could shackle my feet. It was humiliating, him treating me like a wild animal en route to the zoo. I struggled to fight through my emotions.

Once I was loaded in the car, Officer Larson took off in his usual way, racing down side streets, the vehicle's tires groaning as he jerked his sedan around each corner. Despite being restrained by a seatbelt, I had a difficult time maintaining my balance given the shackles. But I didn't say a word. Officer Larson might have been tough, but I would be the bigger man in that exchange. I wouldn't let him break me. That thought provided comfort enough.

I survived the ride. At the new jail in Burleson County, Larson let me out of the car and had me walk, or shuffle, my way into the building. On seeing me, the jailer at the front desk did a double-take as his eyes tracked my body from top to bottom. "Lou," he said, looking at Larson, "was it necessary to hog-tie Graves like that?"

"I'm the one that transported him," Larson said, unfazed by the question. "I have to do it my way."

"Take the damn shackles off his ankles, Lou. He's in the building now."

It wasn't often that jailers stood up for inmates, and I was happy to see Officer Larson called on the carpet. It was a brief respite from the dehumanization inflicted by the system during the transfer process. Larson had me move to a bench and kneel on it while he removed the shackles. Next he removed the handcuffs. The jailer then asked me to follow him down the hall to the shower, where I was asked to strip naked. I was told to run my fingers through my hair, lift up my testicles, turn around and bend over to spread my butt cheeks. Next I was ordered to lift my feet one at a time. Then it was on to the shower for disinfecting from lice and anything else that might have infected us in the darkness and heat of the old jail. I put on the new orange uniform I'd been assigned and was finally escorted to my new cell. The practice reminded me of how the old slave traders had sanitized their human cargo at intake ports in cities like Charleston and Savannah. Or maybe how farmers tended to livestock before the slaughter and subsequent sale. I couldn't decide which, perhaps because it felt like a distinction without a difference. If anyone wants to feel subhuman, be completely stripped of all dignity, and be treated worse than a junkyard dog, go ahead and get arrested in Texas.

The jail wasn't big, but it had the things we'd need to survive day after day. There was B-grade air conditioning and heat, although the jailers set the thermostat, so there was no promise of comfort. The steel beds and benches were no more restful, but at least the metal was shiny and clean. The walls were stark white. You could tell they had just been painted. Even the halls were clean. In that sense, the new Caldwell jail represented a certain upgrade.

My cell itself looked like a fairly large day room. There was a bunk in each corner. The living space was communal. There wouldn't be much privacy for the four of us who shared the room, but we had gotten used to that. Each man had his own toilet, a perk we'd not been afforded in our old haunt. I inspected the desk in my corner. It was small, probably only a couple of feet wide. But it would give me a space where I could write letters to family and friends, or to my lawyer. At this point, Yolanda and I had stopped communicating. It had been a year. She was moving on with her life. Mom was still standing strong, of course, but the rest of my family and friends had started to move on with their lives as well.

None of them knew what to do, how to help me, how to stand up to Charles Sebesta and fight for my freedom, so everyone understandably supported me from a distance. The one exception was Momma, who would visit practically every week, bringing my boys with her when she could. I hated that they had to see their father in jail. It was so unfair. My boys were seven, eight, and eleven. They were victims in this situation too.

Meanwhile, the design of the cell dictated our social interactions. An inmate in search of solitude would rest on his bed or sit at the small metal chair that accompanied his desk. When he wanted to socialize, he'd leave his area behind and pull one of the chairs from under the steel table in the middle of the room. We lived in many ways like college students in a first-year dorm, except there were no trips to the pizza parlor, no beers among friends, nothing that resembled real life beyond our little cages. Fights did break out, but the skirmishes were almost always stress-induced. We were all under pressure, so it was relatively easy to spark a fuse in someone. Most guys, though, spent the bulk of their time in their own space. There would be small tensions around the television, like when someone tried to take control of the remote. One person might want to walk around with the remote in his hand and control what's being watched, and it caused problems but nothing serious that led to any physical altercations. The vibe was cool for me because I was the one usually walking around with the remote. I'd poll the guys to learn what the majority wanted to watch, then I'd implement it evenly so there was no conflict. Everyone felt like there was a fair-enough process most of the time. It helped keep tensions low.

Perhaps most important to me was the phone placed right in our cell. No longer did I have to wait hours for a jailer to stretch that old house phone through the cell's bars. The new phones were expensive, though. Just one fifteen-minute call cost around $6.50. We could purchase calling cards through the commissary. My mom often took her hard-earned money up to the jail so that I could make a call to my family during the week. Every dollar on those cards was precious, allowing me to have contact with my mom and with the world that had been ripped away from me.

Life in the new jail was a little easier because it looked like we were finally headed toward a trial. Calvin visited a handful of times, always asking something new about the case. Eventually I met his colleague Lydia. She asked pointed questions and took copious notes. Though she hadn't tried a capital case either, something about her gave me confidence. She had been with Calvin when they spoke to Sebesta about the direction of my case.

"Anthony," Calvin began at the start of one of our meetings. "Before we proceed, I have something to tell you. You might not want to hear this, but Sebesta has offered you a life sentence."

I was angry. I'd contemplated what a trial might look like, but I hadn't thought about a plea. The gravity of my situation slammed against me when Calvin uttered the word "life." I rejected the offer as quickly as it came.

"You tell Sebesta he can take that life sentence and stick it in his redneck ass. I'm not taking a day for something I didn't do."

"Anthony, listen, you didn't do this." Her words were reassuring. "You don't have to take any deal they offer."

I explained to her that I wasn't going to entertain anything other than my freedom. I had been in jail for more than a year, but I remained resolute. If the state intended to take my freedom, they would have to do it in a trial.

My attorneys must have gotten the message. They quickly tabled the offer. I returned to my cell, smarting at the gall of Sebesta. If he believed I had killed a family, he didn't know me. And if he thought I'd give away my life for a crime I didn't commit, he *certainly* didn't know me.

Sebesta seemed desperate for some piece of evidence he could hang his case on. After all this time, he still had little more than Robert Carter's testimony. Eventually, however, his prodding uncovered something more concrete: a knife. Calvin brought news that Sebesta's find had come from an unlikely source.

"Anthony, Sebesta has taken possession of a knife from your friend Roy Allen," he said. "Sebesta's claiming that the knife matches the stab wounds of the victims." Roy Allen had told investigators that he'd given me the knife's twin from a ceremonial kit he had purchased.

I couldn't believe what I was hearing. I explained to Calvin that the kit knife was so cheap, it had broken within a few months. It wouldn't have been capable of cutting butter, much less murdering someone.

"Well, they seem to think that the knife you had could have been the murder weapon," Calvin said.

Again I saw how the case against me was being crafted out of thin air, with people I knew and items I possessed being squeezed to fit the prosecution's mosaic. The state was working in reverse, starting with the conclusion that I was guilty, then picking through my life for anything that could be made to fit its narrative.

"Get out of here with that," I insisted. "I don't even know where that knife is!"

"Do you think you can find it?" Calvin asked, visibly concerned. He knew that if we could locate the actual knife in question, we could present it as evidence that I had been nowhere near the crime scene. But if we couldn't, then the state might very well use that to grip the malleable minds of the jury. Eventually Calvin calmed down. Maybe he wanted to reassure me.

"It ain't no big deal," he said. "They can't even prove you owned a knife."

I went back to my cell and put pen to paper. The discussion with Calvin had brought back memories of my girlfriend prior to Yolanda, whom I hadn't spoken to in quite some time. She had been around when I had the old knife. I thought that maybe if I got in touch with her, she could put her hands on it. We'd then be able to show just how flimsy the knife was and that it certainly hadn't been used in a rash of killings. I handed my letter to Steve, the jailer I had come to trust. That was a mistake. He delivered it, but not to my ex. He instead took it to Charles Sebesta. I never heard from the girl, and we never found the knife.

Calvin was furious. "Didn't I tell you they couldn't prove you owned a knife?" he asked in a tone I hadn't heard from him before. "Now that you've gone and written a letter that they intercepted, they have proof that you *did* own a knife."

I had wanted to catch the state in a lie, but as it happened, they'd caught me in one. I had testified months earlier that I'd never owned a knife, not intending to mislead anyone. Based on the letter, the state would now be able to paint me as a liar and use that to sway a jury against me.

Calvin urged me not to write any more letters. "Just let it alone!" he said. "They don't have anything on you, and they're grasping at straws."

I assured him I'd let it rest. The last thing I wanted was to help the state in its case against me.

FEBRUARY 1994:
ROBERT CARTER'S TRIAL

· · · · ·

BY THE TIME ROBERT CARTER's case went to trial, in January 1994, I had been in jail for almost a year and a half, and my own case seemed stuck in the mud. Carter's trial promised to get things moving.

I knew the proceedings would weigh heavily on my own. I couldn't be there in person, so I had to rely on my attorney to keep me updated. Every day I imagined what might be happening in the courtroom. Was Sebesta going after Carter like he'd gone after me? What were the witnesses saying? Would they succeed in putting Carter on death row?

The news from Calvin wasn't great.

"During the trial, Scotty testified against Carter," Calvin told me. "He told the court that he heard you and Carter talking. He said Carter admitted to you his role in the murders."

Nothing could have been further from the truth. I was surprised and disappointed in Scotty, but as I look back, I now understand how someone in Scotty's position could look for a way out. I do not blame that on Scotty; I blame it on a criminal justice system set out to win instead of achieving justice. What actually happened is that my interaction with Carter from the time of my arrest had been extremely limited. Apart from my initial plea to him to tell the truth, when I'd been placed across from his holding cell, our only exchanges had occurred just before and after his grand jury testimony, when he'd assured me that he was telling the truth, against his attorney's will and advice, and that his attorney said they'd probably now release me.

Only later did I learn that Carter had testified that *neither* of us had had anything to do with the crime—he'd claimed that he too was innocent.

Now, considering Scotty's lie in court during Carter's trial, I became more concerned. There never was any other conversation between Carter and me beyond this, and there's no way anyone could have heard what Scotty said he'd overheard—because it had simply never happened. If Scotty had lied once in an attempt at making a deal, he might do so again, to my serious detriment.

Meanwhile, my attorney had questions for me.

"Why would Carter have told all those lies about what happened that night?" he asked.

I understood Calvin's purpose in asking the question. He was trying to divine a motive so that he might attack Carter on the stand. And he asked, just as I had asked, because Carter's insistent lies had come screeching out of right field like a baseball flung from some crow-hopper trying to beat a runner at home. I had no connection with Robert Carter. The only reason he knew my name was because of my cousin Cookie, who was seven years older than me. She'd grown up around me and my siblings, but by the time the crime had taken place, we were grown and had moved on with our lives. She had married Carter without my knowledge. At this point, Carter had told a number of conflicting stories. I was hanging on to his grand jury testimony stating that I had nothing to do with the crime. I was confident that he would now stick to the truth, but Calvin, being a defense attorney, wasn't so sure.

There are only so many hours a man can spend thinking about the details of his case. It's only natural to repeat the important plays over and over, like the owner of lost property retracing her steps or a losing quarterback thinking about the throws he might have made. My thinking led me to certain conclusions about the bizarre way I'd been treated in jail. Suddenly I understood why I'd been moved out of the two-man cell with Angel and into an already-occupied space with Scotty. The state wanted information, and they saw my relationship with Scotty as an opportunity to get it. Scotty had been in on the setup.

On February 11, I lay on the floor of my cell waiting on some news of the trial's outcome. Later that day, an officer walked by, a mocking grin on his face. It wasn't strange to see those expressions, but his especially caught my eye. He paused briefly at my door.

"You know they just gave your friend Carter a death sentence?" he asked. "Are you getting scared now?" He chortled and strolled along. The callous way he talked about death was startling. I'm not sure how I expected to feel. I'd never known anyone sentenced to death. As certain as I was about my own innocence, I was that uncertain about his. I hoped he was guilty, because I didn't want to confront the reality that the state might actually execute an innocent man. If Carter was a killer, I was angry to have been linked to him, even in passing by a smirking officer.

I called my attorney. "Calvin, it's Anthony. I just heard from an officer that they convicted Carter and gave him the death penalty."

"Yes, it's true," Calvin said, as if he'd been expecting that very outcome. He told me he'd be in to see me sometime during the week.

I let Calvin know that the officer had taunted me. He told me to hang in there. As if I had any other option.

As it turned out, Carter's case hadn't given us much to go on. Calvin told me that the state had focused almost exclusively on Carter's burn marks. Carter's attorneys had tried to put the crime on me, but the jury still returned a guilty verdict. It wasn't the best news, but Calvin did have something promising to share with me: he had secured a trial date. Calvin and Sebesta would be arguing over my life sometime in October 1994, only six months away.

Calvin explained that I might be brought to court for a few pretrial motions before then. I was grateful that things were beginning to happen. Going to court certainly beat sitting in jail all day. It wouldn't be long until I had an opportunity to prove my innocence, and although that is backwards (the defendant should not have to prove anything), I welcomed the chance. Maybe too much. Back in my cell, thinking about the events to come, I was reminded of something my grandmother had told me when I was a boy. Be careful what you ask for, she'd say, because you just might get it. I'd been asking for a trial, and a trial was what I got.

AUGUST 1994:
TWO YEARS SINCE ARREST

· · · · ·

CALVIN HAD PREPARED ME well for the parade of pretrial motions to come. In the 1990s in Texas, it was up to the defense to make a motion to get information from the prosecution. Our motions would be argued in Brenham, my hometown.

It was a half hour or so from the new Caldwell jail down to Brenham. The route cut across a dusty nowhere, through farmland and a slice of Americana that had been abandoned during the urbanization of Texas. It also passed through Somerville, the scene of the crime for which I stood accused. Momma had told me that the house where the victims had been stabbed and burned was visible from the road. I was as curious as anyone about where it had all gone down, and during the drive to Brenham in August 1994, I searched for a burnt house among the town's other crumbling homes.

Nearly a quarter of Somerville's residents at the time lived beneath the poverty line. Maybe the town had cleaned up the mess after the fire. Perhaps I'd just missed it. I certainly wasn't about to disclose my curiosity to the officer at the wheel. I never did spot the house. The irony was striking. In a few short weeks, I'd be facing the fight of my life. The state would present exacting details on what I'd supposedly done and how I'd done it. And I couldn't even spot the crime scene while driving past it.

I found Calvin waiting at the courthouse counsel table. The transporting officer led me to my seat in handcuffs. Calvin asked that the cuffs be removed. The officer complied. We sat there, waiting on the judge, talking about the details of my case and his expectations for the hearing.

"I've been talking to Sebesta," he said. "He still doesn't know whether Carter will be testifying against you. He says they're still talking to him."

"I hope he does," I told Calvin. "I just can't see that man looking me in the face and lying on me."

"Anthony, I can tell you this," Calvin said in a serious tone, "if they get him to testify, you better believe he'll be testifying *against* you."

As I look back on it, of course it made sense that the DA wouldn't risk putting Carter on the stand unless he knew that his testimony would aid the state's case. But I didn't see it that way at the time. I knew Carter had lied before, but he'd done so in the quiet recesses of back rooms, probably under unthinkable pressure from the Rangers. It was my contention that even if Carter didn't experience some moral renaissance, his conscience would get the better of him if he had to face me in a courtroom.

"Just be prepared, Anthony."

But I wasn't prepared for Calvin's next revelation: Sebesta had been talking about pushing my trial back, to January, after the local elections.

"Look, man, I've been in jail for almost two years," I said, my voice rising in frustration. "If he says he's got a case, then let's go to trial!"

Calvin looked at me blankly, as if he'd conceded the fight for control of the case to Sebesta. It was clear that Sebesta was calling the shots. Calvin had been reduced to a highly paid courier.

I knew we were up against a lot. But I wanted to get on living or dying, and a trial was the only way to do that. I urged Calvin to tell the judge that we were ready to go to trial. He agreed. He would press Sebesta on the earlier trial date.

I knew Calvin was unsure whether he was actually ready to go to trial, and I could sense his trepidation when he spoke in court. It was a big case, a capital murder case. Nevertheless, appearing before the judge, Calvin asked the state to turn over its evidence and contested the change in trial date. In the end, we got everything we wanted: the trial date would remain as assigned and Sebesta was ordered to turn over to us whatever evidence he had.

Before I left the court to return to jail, Calvin stated the obvious: "Don't say anything to the officer on your way back. He'll probably record the conversation. They can and will do anything to gain an advantage over you."

As it happened, we were only a few miles clear of Brenham when the officer transporting me back to jail struck up a conversation. His tone was cordial as he expressed an interest in my case and discussed his version of the facts, asking me the who's and what's and why's. Though remaining quiet was in my best interests, I didn't see much harm in answering his questions, although he seemed to lose interest after a few minutes; maybe he realized my words weren't going to be helpful to whoever had asked him to pick my brain.

Time dragged on in the new jail just as it had in the old. Some cases take a long time to get to trial because the evidence is so complex that lawyers on both sides need to conduct costly investigations. My case lagged for the opposite reason. The statesmen who framed the Constitution weren't explicit enough about the right to a speedy trial, established in the Sixth Amendment. A speedy trial prevents a prosecutor from sitting on a case forever while keeping a defendant jailed and not bringing his or her case to court.

If the prosecution can't make its case within a reasonable amount of time, the defense can ask for a hearing to "calculate" the time. And if, in the eyes of the judge, that period has expired, the defendant's case can be dismissed. In reality, the district attorney almost never lets this happen, since it makes a prosecutor look bad to have time run out. It only works when the DA has lost one of the central witnesses, or if the state never had a case but didn't have the guts to outright dismiss it. Only then will the DA let time expire under speedy-trial rules, so the rule can be blamed rather than the lack of a case.

While Sebesta dragged his feet, my only recourse was to file a costly speedy-trial claim that would take a long time to process and that we stood little chance of winning. These technical maneuvers generally don't win capital murder cases; the system, while supposedly blind, just doesn't allow for that to happen. All it would do is burn more of my days while I sat in jail. The speedy-trial claim was a non-remedy posing as relief, so we never pursued it.

About two weeks after my pretrial hearing, I learned that the circumstances of my detainment would soon be changing. With my trial on the horizon, the state wanted to move me back to the local facility in my hometown of Brenham. On the surface, the plan seemed benign, even charitable. It didn't occur to me at the time that maybe Sebesta was looking to try his luck with a new pool of snitches. The number of mythical conversations attributed to me had grown so large, I'd almost lost count. But the thought of moving closer to my family obscured any downsides.

As it turned out, Washington County Jail wasn't much different than Caldwell. Sitting in my cell at Brenham made me reminisce about the life I'd been away from for two years. I missed the café where I would meet up with Yolanda and the nights we'd spent together. Because I'd always been an upbeat, optimistic person, my mind-set was that things would one day get better for me. I think that's how I was able to stay positive then, and in the long years to come. My approach to life had always been to live until I die, and in between, I would enjoy the time I had.

Now that I was back in my hometown, I realized that I'd been disconnected from more than just the land that made up Brenham. I'd also been disconnected from its people. Most there knew me as the boy who'd pounded doubles into the gap on the baseball diamond and took an extra base when I could. I'd been an athlete, the sort of player blessed with potential that I never fully realized. I'd been outgoing, making friends easily at school and on the streets. My earlier squabble with the law was practically nothing compared to some of the things the police hung on poor black kids in my community. But what did that community think of me now? I hoped maybe Dennis, the guy I met in my holding cell as I was being processed into the new jail, could help me answer that question.

Dennis was in his forties. Though he was older than me, we had some of the same friends in town. Folks who come from small towns pile up far more acquaintances than actual friends. Dennis wouldn't have known much about me back then and even less now. But at the time, he was a rare link to home.

"What's been happening, Dennis?" I asked. When you share suffering, it doesn't take but a minute to open up to people, even if you've only just met. Dennis had been picked up on an outstanding warrant, a consequence of an unpaid ticket of some kind, and here we were together in the same holding cell. He seemed anxious to talk about my case.

"Everybody's shocked these white folks charged you with this crime," he said. "Don't nobody believe this shit." As he spoke his smile turned to a scowl. He asked the obvious question: Why me? I was no closer to an answer than I'd been during any other part of my pretrial detainment.

"Everybody knows you're all about them women, Graves!" There might have been a time when I'd take offense to someone referring to my reputation as a man about town. Certainly I'd earned it. Dennis joked that he might have believed it if they'd charged me with capital heartbreak, but not capital murder. I nodded at him, hoping he spoke for my whole community in seeing me as innocent.

. . . . .

In the weeks prior to my trial, I became dependent upon sources who were less than reliable. A cellmate here. A jailer there. One trusty told me that Sebesta and the Texas Rangers had taken Carter for a drive out to an open piece of land off a country road where Carter had told law enforcement he had hidden the weapons used to murder the Davis family. The Rangers even got divers to search the local lakes. It seemed like a lot to go through to develop a case against an innocent man. Now, I didn't think every law enforcement officer in Texas was out to get me, but I did know that in big cases, they quickly latched on to a suspect—*any* suspect—because that meant they were "doing their job." The alternative is an open multiple-homicide investigation and a "murderer at large" in the community. No public official relishes answering to a city full of scared taxpayers or reading news stories about their incompetence. They liked cases to be investigated and solved, with the perps locked up fast. I was an easy target, with the shoddy testimony of a convicted criminal streamlining their way to a wrong conclusion. After all, who would really fight back? Me? I was poor, black, and powerless, and someone said I did it. That's all it took.

I could never get settled in jail, and maybe that was a good thing. In the period before my trial, it seemed as if I was being moved to a new cell every few weeks. The last of these moves would be to Angleton, in Brazoria County. After the hearing earlier in August, my attorneys had moved for a change of venue, and the judge approved. Capital murder cases typically bring to bear the full force of a community's emotions. Most prosecutors are happy to try cases in the towns where the crime in question took place. Jurors are connected to the community and usually feel a duty to the families of the victims.

I initially thought that the move to Angleton might work in my favor. I hadn't yet come to understand how the criminal law process is designed to advantage the prosecution. The move to Angleton wasn't arbitrary. Sebesta was a skilled venue shopper. He'd moved cases there before with success. His particular brand of law-and-order bravado fit nicely in a town not known for its mercy. Angleton had a history. In 1923, the state conducted its last legal hanging there in the Brazoria County Courthouse. Nathan Lee was a middle-aged black man who was severely mentally disabled. Unable to read or write, he'd signed his own death document with an X. He'd been hanged in a ceremony not too different from the kind Texas uses to kill its citizens on death row today, with the families of the victims and the condemned looking on as witness and sympathizer, and perhaps a member of the press or two to report on the execution. Lee's death might not have been a lynching, but it was close. The Ku Klux Klan famously sent flowers to the funeral of the white man Lee had allegedly killed. In subsequent decades, the killing machine had been well-maintained: Brazoria County had since sent seven men to the death chamber.

Fat droplets of rain plopped onto my head as I walked from the Washington County Jail to the squad car that would carry me to Angleton, a few weeks before my trial. The transporting officer placed my few possessions in the trunk of his police car. For me, this drive was a rare moment of solace. I couldn't really move, my feet being shackled, but I didn't want to. I had heard that filmmakers used rain to signal that a plot change was afoot. If it was good enough for Francis Ford Coppola when he made *The Godfather*, I guessed it was good enough for me.

Brazoria County illustrated the mass incarceration trend of the early 1990s. In 1980, America's federal and state prisons and local jails housed just over 500,000 men and women combined. By 1992, when I was arrested, that number had climbed to almost 1.3 million.* In the two years between my arrest and my entry into Angleton, the United States had somehow added another 170,000 to the ranks of incarcerated Americans. The jail in Angleton was a reflection of that. My cell was overcrowded, bursting beyond capacity. Two inmates slept on the dirty floor, their heads resting on clothes they used to fashion pillows. One slept on the table where we would eat our meals. I felt like the new kid in school when I arrived at the cell door with my standard-issue plastic mattress and pillow. No one was about to give up his spot to make me a bit more comfortable. It felt like a

---

* Nicole Flatow, "Federal Prison Population Spiked 790 Percent Since 1980," *Think-Progress*, February 7, 2013, https://thinkprogress.org/federal-prison-population-spiked -790-percent-since-1980-7d0681772584.

hostel that had conveniently failed to turn off its online reservation system to make up for a few lean months. I wanted a refund.

With our sleeping quarters so tight, I quickly got to know my new neighbors. They vetted my criminal history, not unlike worried landlords renting out a room.

"So, what are you in for?" one of the men asked.

"I'm down here for a trial. They changed my venue and set me up down here." I was deliberately evasive, for obvious reasons.

"Wait, you're the guy they're accusing of killing a whole family," another commented.

Several other faces turned to check me out. Bad news certainly traveled far, even if it hadn't traveled fast. They had heard of me like inmates hear of most things, through snippets of news reports on the television. They told me that Sebesta had been all over the news, proclaiming my guilt to all who would listen. So much for the presumption of innocence. I later learned that it was wrong for him to make such inflammatory statements to the media (something about "poisoning the potential jury pool"), but, then, I'm sure he knew that, just as he also must have known that no one would call him on it.

"Well, he's going to have to bring it on, because I have truth on my side," I said in the toughest voice I could muster. My new friends offered various warnings. Their own experience had taught them that in Angleton, history was always nipping at our heels. Surely they had just wanted to prepare me for what might come. But their words didn't help. I knew good and well what I was up against. Truth may have been on my side, but Angleton's judicial history was strewn with Confederate relics.

OCTOBER 1994:
THE JURY SELECTION

. . . . .

IN MOST CRIMINAL CASES, the jury-selection process is completed in a matter of hours. In capital cases like mine, it can take days or even weeks to choose a jury. Dozens of men and women go through what is in effect an extensive interview process. It's partly so the lawyers can get a sense of whether they'd naturally side with the defense or the state, and if there is some bias that could make them unfit for either side. The other purpose is to determine whether the juror has the capacity to follow the law. Though the system purports to be concerned with potential jurors' understanding of the presumption of innocence, what they're really after is death qualification. In Texas, a juror could not then and cannot now serve on a capital jury unless that juror declares herself capable of applying the death penalty in certain circumstances. It's a process that almost necessarily excludes the bleeding-heart types, if you could rustle any from beneath whatever rocks gave them refuge in a place like Angleton.

As for me and Calvin, our goal was simple. We needed to select twelve jurors and two alternates that would make the state prove my guilt *beyond a reasonable doubt*. Sebesta's goal was different. He wanted jurors who would convict me on sight and be willing to choose death.

I felt all sorts of nausea as I faced the jury pool. I was on display before a group of people who had almost certainly pre-formed some conclusions about my essential character. When Sebesta rose from his chair and started the process, he was all business. Most lawyers use this time to crack a joke or otherwise connect with the group. Some employ strategies to engage potential jurors who look like they'd rather be asleep. I saw none of the latter on my panel. Each candidate seemed willing, anxious even, to captain my fate. They listened intently as Sebesta described the selection process. He was insistent that he had the evidence required to convict me. It took every ounce of restraint I could muster to keep my backside affixed to that court chair. I wanted to jump up and ask him, "What evidence?" knowing he had none.

When Calvin took his turn at getting to know the jurors, he had me stand with him, arm to arm, as a way of humanizing me through an open display of physical contact. I felt stupid. I had words of my own, a story to tell the jury. But at this point, it was up to Calvin to do all the talking as my representative, so I tried to connect with the jurors through eye contact, that old job-interview tactic. I set my gaze on one individual after another. One man looked away, another stared down. I attached meaning to everything. Maybe they were averting their gaze because I scared them. Perhaps they looked away because their minds were made up. It did my mind no good to worry, but that didn't stop me from chasing those questions down rabbit trails. I resigned myself to the terrifying reality that I'd have to prove those jurors wrong, even though I technically didn't have the burden of proof.

The jurors were white, for the most part. There was only one person on the jury who shared my skin tone, and he was picked to be the foreman. It became apparent just how steep my climb might be.

Juror questioning was curious to me. Sebesta gave a handful of panel members the chance to speak their minds about the justice system. Some of the questions were simple; some seemed like tests to determine a juror's bias.

"I don't think he would be here if he hadn't done something," one juror said. More than one person said they felt that most young blacks were criminals. Pressed to explain, one man said, "When I see blacks approaching my car, I have the tendency to lock my car doors."

I was like a fly buzzing from stop to stop on some antebellum porch, where the genteel class talked about how scary I looked. In another setting, it might have been an entertaining portal to an earlier time. But in that court, my life was on the line. Still, I was happy to hear the answers. Better an open racist than a quiet one, or so I thought. This juror had given his version of the truth, a brave showing of transparency that would surely see him off my jury. But I winced as I then watched that juror redeemed through a process called "rehabilitation." The judge asked questions of him that couldn't have possibly uncovered the truth.

"I hear what you're saying, but do you think you can follow the law in this case?" the judge asked.

It took only a nod and a subtle grunt that sounded like a yes to "rehabilitate" this juror. He'd given the game away, admitting that for him, the presumption of innocence could never hold. Yet one question from the judge had restored his eligibility to serve. It struck me that this form of so-called rehabilitation was no better than releasing a drunk with a beer in his hand on the promise that he'd pour it out when he left the facility. Calvin looked at me, questioning my opinion about his eligibility. I didn't hesitate.

"Strike his ass!" I said. Before too long, we were out of our peremptory challenges, the strikes we could use without offering a reason to the court. The law only gives each side so many peremptory challenges to ding potential jurors, and rehabilitated racists outstripped our allotted exclusions. The judge had the discretion to grant additional challenges. He chose not to, however, and the jury pool took on an unsavory cast.

Meanwhile, a review of juror questionnaires led to the elimination of nearly every black person on hand. In a back room, I watched as they were excused in turn for one problem or another. The Supreme Court's holding in *Batson v. Kentucky* was supposed to guarantee a defendant a fair trial with a jury composed of his peers by prohibiting a peremptory challenge to a juror on the basis of race, gender, or ethnicity. In reality, making "Batson challenges," as they are called in practice, that jurors were being excused because they were black, did little to usher a few more brothers onto my jury. At the time in Somerville, where the crime had taken place, the US Census gauged that just over 30 percent of the citizens were black. On my jury, only a single black man was invited to join with eleven white men and women.

The jury results were disheartening. I didn't know the jurors, but the way they looked at me made me feel like an interloper in my own case.

Calvin left me to find out who the jury had picked as its foreman. As though it mattered. I assured him that it would be the black man. He looked at me curiously and pushed back from his chair. I waited patiently for him to return, thinking of all the different ways to say "I told you so."

"Well, you were right," he said when he rejoined me in the courtroom. "It's the black guy."

The newly minted foreman was the head of the snake. If they were going to convict me, then the lone black juror would be the face of it all. I questioned whether he could stand up to the pressure of eleven white folks if it came down to that. Hell, it was entirely possible that he'd lead the charge. Very serious people told me the system was designed to uncover the truth, to get it right. My challenge was to empower my heart, which believed that sentiment, over my mind, which saw the cracks in the system, flaws that could cost me my life.

Trials are mostly a game of hurry up and wait. Once the jury was selected, I retired to my cell. Sebesta's strategy was clear: control the narrative. The trial hadn't even begun, yet he was intent to make his case in the local media. Typically, he was given a time slot and handed a microphone to deliver his monologue uncontested. Nobody seemed interested in the quality of the state's case. "Anthony Graves is guilty of this heinous crime," he'd say, as if speaking directly to the jurors. To my surprise, the only people who seemed alarmed by the prosecutor's words were sitting in jail cells beside me. Calvin assured me that Sebesta could talk all he wanted in front of the cameras. We would do our talking in court.

The reality of what I was up against slammed into me like a rogue wave off the Gulf Coast. I used short, repeatable phrases to calm my nerves and restore my confidence, the audible equivalent of stroking rosary beads. *They can't do no more to me than what God lets them do,* I would repeat, like a mantra, and *The truth will come out and I'll have the last laugh.* My saving grace was my attitude. They could not make me guilty even if they convicted me, and that made me right all the time.

This time, I had to put my trust in Calvin. I repeated to myself, over and over, *Calvin has a plan, Calvin has a plan.* My lawyer was all that I had.

Those thoughts kept me going. I held an unwavering faith that no matter how cunning a prosecutor might be, his legal hijinks could not overpower the principles of American democracy. The ability to hold onto hope rested with me alone; I had control over that, and it was one of the few things Sebesta couldn't steal from me. This might have been a naive belief, and yet it saved my life.

At the same time, I was aware of the systemic bias that existed in Texas against young black men like me. I had witnessed it dozens of times on the streets of my own community. On any given night, you could pretty much bet on seeing a uniformed white man, hand on holster, taking out the cuffs, shouting aggressively at a black or brown person standing against a car, wall, or fence. But I hadn't known that the criminal justice system would sanction law enforcement officers picking me up from my home and putting me in jail for a capital crime on the basis of false testimony, without a shred of evidence. I wouldn't have believed it was possible that our legal system was capable of that kind of barbarism.

I spent most of my time in the days leading up to my trial sitting on the steel table in the Angleton cell, watching television or lying in bed reading books. Sometimes I would play dominoes at the table with some of the guys. I had begun to pick up a few pounds by this time in jail and was now weighing in at about 166 pounds, nearly 10 more than when I'd arrived. I could feel my body starting to change. My energy level wasn't as high. I was just going with the flow of the day in a cell that now felt very caged in to me. I had nothing to wake up to anymore, except for trial days, and those were emotionally draining. I carried heavy bags under my eyes to court each morning. Calvin had more on his mind than just picking that jury. He had been pressing the state for information on the witnesses the prosecution planned to call. The big question was clear: would Robert Carter testify? Sebesta continued to toy with Calvin, maintaining that Carter's story was shifting. The state claimed it didn't know and couldn't know whether Carter would be called to the stand.

OCTOBER 1994:
MY TRIAL BEGINS

· · · · ·

AN ODD CALM SETTLED over me the morning of October 20, 1994, the opening day of trial. I had been waiting more than two years for my day in court, and it was finally here.

Calvin approached as I sat patiently in the holdover, a small cell set off from the courtroom by a large wooden door. "Anthony, I've just spoken with Sebesta," he said. "Carter has agreed to testify for the state."

I repeated what I had told Calvin many times before. State's witness or not, Carter wasn't going to lie about me to my face. Calvin didn't share my confidence. He tried to prepare me for what he viewed as an inevitability. Sebesta wouldn't be putting Carter on the stand unless he was confident his testimony would help the state's case. As a defense lawyer, Calvin had seen people lie on the stand. I listened to him, but in my idealism I continued to believe that one look at my face in that courtroom would break Carter's will and stir his conscience.

Calvin urged me to prepare myself. "Anthony, I want you to remember this," he said. "As Carter testifies, no matter what he says, do not shake your head. Do not show any physical reaction. Don't do anything that the jury can misinterpret. Just sit still and listen. Take notes if you need to, but don't show any visible reaction."

I assured him that I would remain composed. I knew from his expression that Calvin was concerned, even anxious. But before I had time for any further consult with my attorney, I found myself being led into court through that same large door.

I was wearing crisp gray slacks, a starched white shirt pulled tightly across my chest, and a defiant red tie, the color of the fiery shirt Tiger Woods confidently wore during the final rounds of major golf tournaments, in an attempt to urge himself to victory. My blazer was blue with shiny buttons. I felt comfortable in those clothes. They were smart and tailored. My hair, however, was not. Calvin had made what I considered a strange request. He asked that I not cut my hair. His reasoning was that he didn't want the jury to think I was trying to alter my appearance. I felt certain that with my hair disheveled, I looked like a homeless man who had somehow stumbled upon a suit.

The courtroom was sparsely decorated. A large, bronze-colored star was affixed to one wall. Pictures of ambiguously important men dotted the wall opposite it. There were large tables for the lawyers, while a sprawling bench housed seats for the judge and the witnesses. It felt as though the entire room was against me. Like the football team that looks to its loyal fans in the visitor's section, I sought out the comfort of familiar faces. Nearly everyone close to me was there—my mom, my brothers and sisters. Most of them just smiled. I nodded back reassuringly. One family friend that I had known for many years went through a series of hand signals, making not-quite-closed fists at ten and two, as if she was steering an invisible wheel. When she pointed at me, I knew what her motions were saying. I'd be driving them home when the trial was through. I imagined it as if it was real. Driving them home might lead to the comfort of my bed or a little couch-sitting with my family after hugs with my mother. I wanted to roughhouse with my sons and talk to them about their lives. I wanted what I had before, and if I had another chance, I knew I would appreciate it in ways most people don't think about until they lose something precious.

Sebesta began the trial in the same way he'd begun my bail hearing. He called to the stand the fire marshal, who once again described the gruesome crime scene. The fire marshal talked of charred bodies and lingering smoke, of the inexorable smells. He described how he could tell that the fire was started intentionally—something to do with burn patterns. As he spoke, I wondered whether he was right. I knew that the state's witnesses were lying about my involvement or wouldn't be able to point to me at all, but I didn't, at the time, know much about the appearance of the crime scene or the evidence that had been found there. I considered whether the marshal had actually stumbled upon the scene he described, whether his testimony was a nugget of truth or just another in a long line of lies in support of a forgone conclusion.

The state next called a jailer from Caldwell. Calvin had warned me that it might be difficult to hear people lie about me on the stand. I did my best to mute my reactions when false testimony cascaded through the courtroom.

"What did you hear the defendant say?" Sebesta asked.

"He said, 'Shut the fuck up! I did the job for you!'" the jailer responded. I wanted to stand up and yell bullshit. I wanted to explain to the jury that in the old Caldwell jail, the creaky fan, yelling inmates, and intermittent television made it so loud that even if I had wanted to communicate with Carter, I'd have had to yell at the top of my voice to do so.

Calvin started in on the jailer, hoping to cast aspersions on his dubious story. "Have you ever heard Mr. Graves speak?" he asked.

"Well, I guess not," the jailer said. It felt like a win. The jailer had admitted that he was in no position to know what my voice sounded like. He would later admit that the intercoms in the cells were faulty and only worked on occasion. Sometimes the intercom would play audio from Cell 7 while the light indicated that the noise was coming from Cell 9, and so on. The jailer seemed to be working from a script. He quickly took the chance to tell the jury he had tried to record the conversation. His efforts had conveniently failed.

Calvin revealed on cross-examination that the jailer had failed to file a report until many weeks after the alleged conversation. He had, however, filed a detailed report that same night, recalling for posterity that he had given an inmate an aspirin. I looked to the jury to see how they took the news. It didn't seem as if they were finding fault in this cast of characters. They listened intently as if the next sentence might clear up the contradiction.

It must have been Sebesta's belief that if he couldn't get one witness to tell the truth about my time in Caldwell jail, then he could get two half-truths or even three third-truths to add up to one truth. He called two more witnesses, both officers, who testified that they too had heard me at different times talk to Robert Carter about my involvement in the murders. To hear them tell it, I was at once a seasoned criminal, using words to intimidate Carter, and a buffoon, someone stupid enough to admit in a room full of people looking for a way out that I had done the crimes. Caldwell was full of men looking for relief. You'd have to be crazy or suicidal to implicate yourself in front of those willing snitches. I was neither, but it didn't seem to matter much.

A familiar face came to the stand next—an ex-girlfriend I had been missing when I was arrested at the beginning of this nightmare. I watched as she walked down the aisle, entered the well, and took the witness stand. Even though she appeared as a name on the witness list, I wondered why they might be calling her. I hadn't been with her in a long time. We'd broken up a few months before the murders.

"Did the defendant keep a knife in your apartment?" Sebesta asked her.

My heart sank as I remembered the intercepted letter I'd written to her earlier in the summer.

She said that I did, but that I hadn't carried it on my person. Sebesta held up the souvenir knife that he'd gotten from Roy Allen. He put on quite a production, moving the knife from hand to hand while looking intently at its impotent blade. That knife had been tested by Ranger Ray Coffman, or so the state claimed. Coffman took the stand and testified that the knife's blade was consistent with the wounds of the victims, despite not being an expert on knives, as I would later learn. He moved the knife up and down as he described how the blade matched the puncture wounds in the skull of one of the children. This testimony should have been challenged or disallowed, as again Coffman was not, nor could he have been, qualified as an expert on knives, but I learned all of this too late.

Coffman looked at the jury as he paused for dramatic effect. "Like a glove," he said. "It fit like a glove."

The knife became a central prop as it was passed from lawyer to lawyer, witness to witness. Coffman held it closely on the stand, extending it on occasion to draw the jury's attention. I knew it wasn't the murder weapon, of course. It wasn't even a replica of the murder weapon. It was the twin of the cheap blade I'd long ago been given by a friend. But as the Ranger waved it around, it was clear that the jury was fixated.

During his cross-examination, Calvin approached the stand with an array of knives he and Lydia had purchased to make their point. Calvin presented each of these knives, all similar in size to the knife in the state's custody, to the jury, claiming that they too were consistent with the victims' puncture wounds. To demonstrate, Calvin held in his hand the actual skull cap of one of the victims. Like a macabre magician, he plunged the various blades into the holes representing puncture wounds. Each knife fit perfectly, despite their different appearances. The point, it seemed, was to demonstrate what experts would (many years) later conclude: almost any knife of equivalent size would conform to the holes in that skull. Though my attorney was allowed to test the fit in the skull wounds to challenge Coffman's testimony about the knife, it may have done more harm than good to continue to present those sickening images and references to the gruesome murders. Regardless, this paled in comparison to keeping the non-expert knife testimony off the stand, which is what should have happened in a proper legal defense.

Calvin also argued to the jury that the knife presented to the state, weak and flimsy as it was, made for an unlikely murder weapon. Of course, I don't know whether Roy's knife or the twin he gave me could have cut through a human skull. It wouldn't have occurred to me to put it to the test. I do recall that knife having a hard time cutting its way through butter, and it broke so soon after I got it that I had to question Roy's gift-giving skills.

The testimony surrounding the knife had surely been dramatic. The question was, what would the jury make of it?

Listening to the proceedings, I was convinced that the state's case, though sensational, wasn't strong. The prosecution needed Robert Carter's testimony. And I was holding on to the belief that Carter, when face to face with me in the courtroom, would be compelled to tell the truth, as he had before the grand jury.

You've got to see the good in a man, I thought to myself. *There's some honor in everyone, even those the state has sentenced to die.*

. . . . .

It seemed to take forever for Robert Carter to walk to the stand. He looked down, never breaking stride to glance at me or the jury. I was happy to see him. I just wanted to look him in the eye. I fixed my eyes on him, studying the contours of his face as he settled in to speak. He never returned my stare.

Sebesta started with the basic questions before moving on to the meat of Carter's testimony. My anticipation built as the DA began digging in to Carter's recollection of the night of the murders.

Carter spoke in a low monotone as he confessed what he had done. I hung on his every word until the words fell from his mouth with impressive torque: "Graves and I committed the crime."

I fought a sense of shock. Deep down, I'd known it was possible that he might say just that, but as a survival tactic, I hadn't let myself believe it, even though my attorney had sought to prepare me for this very outcome. My eyes blurred as the room zoomed in and out of focus.

Sebesta followed Carter's claims with a simple request. "Is that man in the courtroom today? Can you point him out for the record?"

For the first time, Carter barely glanced my way. He extended the index finger of his right hand, pointing in my general direction. I felt like I'd been punched in the gut. With the speed of some shamed admirer who'd been caught fawning for too long, he looked away. He wasn't going to tell the truth. In fact, his lies had grown bolder, his testimony placing me at the center of the murders.

My belief in the goodness of the system was underpinned by my belief in the goodness of men. Carter smashed all of that. The system was exposed as a beast just as flawed as the humans it depends on. I felt the tangible weight of hopelessness. I wore it like a blanket, or worse, a straitjacket. Carter continued to speak, and I couldn't do a thing in my defense. In fact, doing anything would have enhanced the effect of the words he spoke.

"I finally came into the house where Graves was and all I could see was blood. There was blood everywhere."

I didn't envy Calvin's task as he cross-examined Carter. Of course, there was room to do so. But Carter's statements had saddled the courtroom with a certain heft. Calvin trudged on.

"Mr. Carter, haven't you given many different versions of your story to investigators?"

This, of course, was a fact. Carter had spun quite a few yarns in the two years since the murders were committed. In one of his tall tales, from his fourteen-hour interrogation with the Texas Rangers on the day of his arrest, he'd said I killed the family because I wanted to have sex with one of the victims. In another, my motive was less sinister—Carter said I was taking revenge against Bobbie Davis, one of the victims, for being promoted to a job my mother was passed over for. Carter made up a total of seven different stories on the night that he was first interrogated. The Rangers picked the story that they felt they could best build a case around. Clearly, Carter was willing to say or do anything in the hope of being released.

Calvin pulled from his folder a trump card. It was the grand jury testimony in which Carter told those members that he had acted alone, something we confirmed by gaining access to his grand jury testimony in preparation for trial. Carter read it aloud. Calvin was satisfied. He excused Carter right then and there. I couldn't believe it. I'm not sure what more I wanted Calvin to ask, but there *had* to be more. I started scribbling. I wanted him to ask Carter how we knew each other. Where did we hang out? Where was our meet-up place on the night of the crime? Calvin could have asked him anything about me, and if Carter answered correctly, it would only have been the result of a very good guess. Those questions went unasked and unanswered as Carter stood, adjusted his shirt, and ambled off the stand. When Calvin returned to our table, I pushed my questions in his direction. "Call him back and ask him these questions," I whispered.

"Anthony, we just want to hurry up and get Carter off the stand."

"He doesn't know me," I said.

"Don't question the legal strategy," Lydia chided.

I was no longer sure Calvin *had* a legal strategy. I felt a little like a deckhand asking a captain why he'd cut loose a trophy-sized catch. I wasn't the expert, after all. Maybe there was something that Calvin planned to introduce later that would bring it all together, make sense of it all. At this point, there was nothing I could do. He was my attorney; he must have known what he was doing, right? If I didn't have faith in my attorneys, where would I be? They were all I had, and I had to believe they knew best how to defend me. I'd wanted Carter grilled long and hard, and exposed for what he was—a lying piece of shit. It didn't go down that way in court, and I could only hope that there was a reason for that.

With Carter's exit, the state rested its case. I imagined what I might be thinking if I were sitting in the jury box. I imagined the jury box filled with reasonable people, and I hoped those reasonable jurors might see through the implausible jailers, the flimsy knife, and the ever-changing chronicles of Robert Carter.

Calvin had been thrown off by Carter's latest story. We had prepared for a version that included a trip to the gas station. After all, the state had called me in for a lineup those many months ago. Sebesta presumably had an eyewitness willing to testify that she had seen me filling a gas can on that night. But when Carter stated on the stand that he already had the gas when he picked me up, Calvin wasn't sure where to go. Our mistake was in trusting that a liar might stick to one lie. Sebesta had cleverly manipulated Carter to move the goalposts after Calvin spent weeks preparing to combat the gas station identification.

After the state rested its case, it was our turn. Calvin called a man named John Isom to the stand. Isom thought his cousin Keith could have been involved in the crime. Keith's daughter Denitra—Lisa Davis's eldest child and half-sister to Carter's son Jason—was one of the victims. Isom had seen Keith the night of the murders and thought he had acted strangely. For us, Isom's role was simple. Jurors are human at their core. They don't want to believe there are murderers roaming the streets. Shrewd defense attorneys understand that when you present the "I Didn't Do It" defense, you must give jurors a plausible alternative. In this case, the jurors believed that Robert Carter was involved, either as the main actor or an accomplice. Sebesta had been convincing in his argument that the crime had involved two perpetrators. We needed to present a viable theory to the jury.

"Did your cousin come to your house on the night of the murder?" Calvin asked.

"He did," Isom said. "He came and I consoled him because his daughter had been one of the victims. He seemed almost unaffected, as if he was indifferent. Maybe he was in shock, but something didn't seem right." Isom went on to say that his cousin Keith left the house abruptly when he'd stepped out of the room for a minute.

We next called Wanda Lattimore to the stand. Carter had testified on direct examination earlier in my trial that I killed Bobbie Davis and her family because Bobbie had beaten out my mom for a job promotion. I had to have some motive, after all, if I was going to kill six people. That story was the state's college try.

Wanda was my mom's supervisor. "The two of them worked very well together," she said on direct examination, referring to my mother and Bobbie Davis. "They certainly got along." She also testified that my mother had never applied for the job in question. This seemed to dispense with any "revenge" motive on my part, but I questioned whether that would matter to the jury. Calvin had told me that the state doesn't have to prove motive. It only helps to fill in any gaps that jurors might have. I wondered if Wanda's testimony would be of any help to me.

I watched the jurors carefully. One man fidgeted with his glasses. A woman adjusted the shoulder pad of her shirt incessantly. I had become a master of observation, noticing and remembering details, because it was details that would save my life. I remembered perfectly the things I did, the words I said, and the food I ate on the night the crimes were committed. As my brother Arthur walked toward the witness stand, I wondered whether his memory was as clear as mine.

Arthur recalled that we'd all shared my mother's apartment that night. He remembered the greasy brown bags of fast-food sandwiches we'd brought home. He even testified to the ribbing he sustained when I caught him cooing to his lady friend, Kaye, on the telephone. His memory was flawless. He painted for the jury a scene that was so routine, so mundane, it would qualify as unpublishable fiction had he made it up. His last words stuck with me. He spoke quickly and smoothly when he told the jury exactly how Yolanda and I were positioned on our floor pallets. He motioned with his hands like a builder explaining where various pieces might go. He had stepped over us, he said, recalling our sleeping bodies like immovable Tetris pieces on his way to lock the front door.

A series of witnesses followed Arthur. Yolanda's dad, Bubba, recalled his girlfriend Bernice offering to babysit so that we could enjoy a night away. Bernice echoed his claims, recalling even more detail about the route we'd taken when we picked her up from work. They couldn't testify to my whereabouts after Yolanda and I left them, of course, but their stories lined up with Arthur's and those of the other witnesses.

The success of our case presentation turned more on what wasn't said than what was. I'd learn later that Sebesta had investigated our phone records, hoping to find a call from Robert Carter to the residence. That never materialized. Calvin missed his chance too. He might have pulled the call log to prove that Arthur had actually spoken to Kaye in that clownish conversation. He didn't do it, and we missed out on Kaye's testimony too. She originally planned to testify on my behalf, to tell the court that late that night, I'd given her the most benign kind of trouble on the phone. But her feet cooled. Her family was racist, she said, and she could never have her dad know that she'd been on the phone with a black man late at night.

Kaye wasn't the only witness to go AWOL. As Calvin prepared to call Yolanda to the stand, Sebesta jumped from his seat.

"Who do you intend to call next?" he asked. The question seemed odd given that each witness we called or planned to call was on the witness list that we'd provided him.

"I plan to call Yolanda Mathis," Calvin said. Yolanda's testimony was important, and not just because she'd slept close enough to me to feel my body heat the night I was supposedly involved in a murderous rampage. The fact that she had a boyfriend at the time that we were seeing each other worked to my advantage. It lent her credibility, being that she had no incentive to lie to protect me. Precisely the opposite, in fact. Testifying on my behalf would open Yolanda up to character assassination and might lead to consequences in her relationship. She would be testifying against her own interests, one of the legal hallmarks of veracity. She'd known this going in but had still agreed to take the stand in my defense.

Sebesta addressed the judge directly. "Your honor, we need to excuse the jury for a short recess. I have something for the record."

I looked to Calvin, my head cocked and eyes squinted as I sought guidance on what was going down. My attorney shrugged, clearly puzzled himself about what the DA was up to.

Once the jury was cleared from the room and well out of earshot, Sebesta announced to the court, incredibly, that "Yolanda Mathis is now a suspect in this murder." He continued, "Before she gives testimony in this case, she should be read her Miranda rights." He told the judge that there was a strong possibility that Yolanda would be indicted for capital murder. My eyes widened at the prosecutor's incredible statement, right there in open court. Calvin's shock exceeded my own. He asked for a recess, so we could all leave the courtroom and regroup in private. Before the recess was granted, Calvin asked for a minute to relay the message. As a defense attorney, he had a duty to inform Yolanda of what had happened because she wasn't represented by counsel. I sat alone at our table as Calvin left to break the news to her in the witness room adjacent to our courtroom. Calvin came back and told me that Yolanda began to shake at the news, and tears rushed down her face. Calvin told me she ran from the courtroom and clear out of the courthouse.

Court was still in session when he returned. "The witness has decided not to testify," Calvin told the court in a sidebar with the judge so as to be outside of jurors' hearing. "She has invoked her Fifth Amendment rights."

The Fifth Amendment states that a person can refuse to testify on the grounds that something they say may be used to incriminate them. In other words, you can't be forced to become a possible witness against yourself. It's just plain easier, and legally smarter, to refuse to say anything when you are told you are a suspect in a capital murder case, regardless of whether you had anything to do with it. You just can't take the risk that something you say might somehow be twisted against you. Once she'd been named a suspect, Yolanda had little choice but to take the Fifth. In the end, this was merely a trial tactic by an overzealous prosecutor trying to win at all costs. Sebesta was trying to intimidate Yolanda against taking the stand, since she would have been a credible witness in my favor, and his efforts worked as planned. There was never any evidence against her, and she was never ultimately charged. It was all just part of the game.

As the court proceedings continued, the expressions on my attorneys' faces told a story I didn't want to read. Yolanda was our star witness and now she was gone. I summoned positivity because it beat the alternative. I held out the hope that my brother's detailed testimony about my whereabouts that night had been enough to satisfy the jury.

Sebesta's closing argument would haunt me during the long nights spent on death row. He had manipulated Yolanda, scaring her into silence with empty threats. We'd find out long after the trial that the DA had never previously named her as a suspect. It was all just a ploy, a veritable chess move that put us in checkmate. But the prosecutor wasn't content simply to sabotage our case. He would use Yolanda's absence to bolster his own. Rising from his chair to begin his grand salvo, the DA all but pranced around the room, his eyes shifting from the jury to me and back again.

"Ladies and gentlemen of the jury," he said. "Mr. Graves claims he was with someone that night. Where is this alibi witness? Why wasn't she here to testify?" The jury never learned that Yolanda Mathis had fully intended to testify but had run from the courthouse that day out of fear of being charged with a crime. And why wouldn't she be afraid? She'd been with me that night, so she knew firsthand my whereabouts at the time of the murders. She knew I was innocent, and that the state was railroading an innocent person. What would stop Sebesta from going after her? I couldn't blame Yolanda. Sebesta didn't care about innocence or guilt. He just wanted a conviction. His zealousness was matched only by his reckless disregard for the truth.

OCTOBER 27–NOVEMBER 1, 1994:
THE JURY MAKES A DECISION

· · · · ·

THE WAITING IS THE WORST. An officer walked me back to the adjacent jail. There, I ate a sandwich and listened as two officers discussed my case like fans chewing over the first half of a football game.

"What do you think, man?" one of them said.

"I don't know," the other responded. "They didn't prove anything to me."

I agreed, of course, but they didn't seem to care much what I thought.

My imagination churned as the jury went about its business in an adjacent room. I could hear them moving around every so often, the bottoms of their chairs scraping the hard floor. I heard the toilet flush as they took their bathroom breaks. Occasionally they raised their voices. Sometimes they'd be very quiet. It struck me that a raised voice meant someone was yelling about me, about my life. I wondered what the quiet meant. Had they decided my fate? My confidence slowly eroded over the course of nine hours. I prepared for the worst. I wanted to believe in them, but I had heard too much during the selection process. For days, eleven white jurors had listened to a white prosecutor point the finger at a black man they didn't know. I'd been dehumanized, made into the bogeyman they needed to fear. It was going to be hard for this jury in this town to return a not-guilty verdict. I figured they couldn't do it, and even if they could, they wouldn't. The hours ticked, and I watched the clock. It was like when I was a kid, waiting for Momma to get home after I'd done something wrong. You just knew she'd make you pick out your own switch.

Finally, the jury buzzed the bailiff to let the court know that they'd reached a verdict. Officers escorted me back to the defense table where I had spent the last week. I watched closely as the jurors entered the room. Several of the women were crying, their faces weathered from the preceding task. Maybe it had been harder on them than I thought. Calvin must have seen the same thing. He leaned over to speak.

"What do you think, Anthony? How do they look to you?"

"You've seen how they talked about folks who look like us," I said. "They determined my fate a long time ago." There was no doubt in my mind that they had come back with a guilty verdict. I was mentally exhausted and just wanted to get this part over with.

The foreman informed the judge that the jury had indeed reached its verdict. The bailiff approached the foreman and took possession of the piece of paper that held my fate. They all pretended the outcome was some great mystery. The judge shot the paper a passing glance.

"Mr. Garvie, will you and your client please stand?" the judge asked. I wasn't afraid. An unlikely peace shrouded me. I had told the truth, and that was all I could do. My lawyers were green, but they'd worked hard and believed in me. It was a surreal resignation.

"Mr. Graves," the judge said, "a jury of this court has found you guilty of capital murder." Calvin shook his head, his movements a little faster with each oscillation. A waterfall erupted from his eyes.

"This is not right, this is not right, this is not right." He muttered those words again and again for what seemed like minutes. I couldn't react. I thought about the inevitability of it all. I thought about the trial that had taken place, and how I never really stood a chance in that courtroom.

That an innocent black man was convicted wasn't a bug in the system, I knew. It was a feature of it.

· · · · ·

Back at the jail, I just wanted some alone time. Avoiding contact, I went to where phone booths sat empty, awaiting prisoners making calls to their attorneys or families. I found a metal bench. It felt like every room I'd been in for the last two years had a metal bench. I stared forward. When I was arrested, I had rubbed my head, hoping it was all a dream. My reaction after the verdict was something similar. We had focused much of our attention on the guilt-innocence phase of my trial. Now my lawyers had to worry about saving my life. The same phrase kept running through my head: *These people are trying to kill me.* And it seemed they were succeeding. What about my children? What about my mom?

I slowly got up from the metal bench and walked into my cell to lay down on my bunk. I didn't get back up until the next morning to go back to court. It was a long night.

The punishment phase got started the following Monday. The same officers who'd chewed the fat over my case the day before escorted me into the courtroom. I was the last to enter. The families of the victims sat quietly. Calvin and Lydia sat at the defense table. Sebesta was there, employing a winning swagger.

While the guilt-innocence phase of my trial had been an inquisition into the facts of the crime, the sentencing phase was an appraisal of me. The jury had a simple but weighty task: decide whether I was worth keeping alive. In Texas, this process means an exploration of aggravating and mitigating circumstances. The state's goal was to paint me as dangerous, unredeemable, subhuman. Calvin was charged with convincing jurors who had just convicted me of murder that I had redeeming qualities. The first state's witness was Tommy Genzer, the former foreman at the plant where I worked. We had been close friends. I could tell that he didn't know he was there to testify in favor of the prosecution. It quickly dawned on him.

"Mr. Genzer, could you please tell us about an incident Mr. Graves had with another employee at work?" Sebesta was talking about an altercation I'd been involved in many years before. A coworker had slapped me, and when I hit back, I'd broken his nose. Sebesta wanted my foreman to talk only about what I had done, and not about why the fight started. All of a sudden, a scrap among friends took on a different character. To the jury, which had already decided that I was capable of mass murder, the seemingly innocuous fight revealed a pattern of violence.

Texas Ranger Earl Pearson came next. He talked about the crime scene and the effect it had on him. He said he'd lost sleep over it, a fact I don't doubt. He said that he had to check up on his children as they slept in the days and weeks following the crime. It sounded scary. I thought about my three boys. I knew the jury would be doing the same with their own kids.

I drifted to thoughts of all that I was missing. My boys were just starting to get into sports when I was arrested. I missed seeing them trying their best on the ball field. I missed seeing them on my visits and hanging out with them during the summers when school was out. I missed staying on my oldest son Terrell about his homework, and the little stubborn attitude he was developing. I missed staying overnight with him at the hospital when his sickle-cell anemia got bad. Until my arrest, as his father, it was important for me to be there for him during the hard times.

With my middle son Terrance, I missed going out to the country. His mother's side of the family called him Donut. They lived about fifteen miles outside the city limits of Brenham. We called it the Country. I would go out there and hang out with him and his family on the weekends. Country people knew how to enjoy life. His grandpa would be cooking stuff like rabbit and 'coon. I had never tasted wild food like that in my life. It was good though. I used to go out there hoping his grandpa had cooked some rabbit, and I would find them barbecuing and playing dominoes under the tree. My son's grandpa would be playing blues music from the trunk of his car, while my little bucket-head son would be running around playing with his cousins and enjoying life.

My youngest son, Alex, was the shy one. Alex wouldn't say two words to anybody. His own mother would have to make him talk to her. He would drive me crazy by not telling someone when he had to use the bathroom. I was at work one day when I got a call from the school asking if I could come pick Alex up. This boy had pooped his pants and had the whole front office lit up with a horrible smell. When I got there, he looked at me all quiet with big eyes. I asked him why he didn't tell the teacher he had to use the bathroom. I took him home to his mother with the car windows rolled down. This little boy did things like that, and he was a light in my life. He was sweet and innocent, and a funny boy who made me laugh and laugh and laugh. I missed being with him.

I also missed my ex-girlfriend's daughter, Echo. I'd grown to be like a father to her during the time I dated her mother. We had bonded over the years as father and daughter and no one knew the difference. She'd had a habit of waking up early on Saturday mornings on the weekends her mother had to work to ask me if we could go to McDonald's for breakfast. I didn't know how she knew which weekends her mother would have to work, but it never failed. And I'd always go get her.

Terrell, Terrance, Alex, Echo—I missed them all. But reality was staring me in the face, and the hearing continued.

The state's sentencing case shifted rapidly from the horrific nature of the crime to the horrific nature of me, the man apparently responsible for it. In 1994, the Texas legal system was very much concerned with the concept of "future dangerousness." A so-called future-dangerousness test was employed at this stage of the trial. Jurors were asked to consider whether I posed a future threat to society. It was a distinction that seemed odd given that the alternative to death was life in prison without the possibility of parole. It also seemed like an elusive notion. Sebesta understood the value of framing difficult-to-grasp issues through the lens of science. That's why he called a psychiatrist to talk about the threat that I might pose to society. Dr. Walter Quijano had never met me, never even spoken to me. He made grand claims about the nature of my character as jury members looked upon him with a sort of unquestioning adulation. The irony shook me in my seat. I peered at Sebesta, thinking only that here he was asking questions about my future dangerousness when he was the one asking jurors to kill an innocent man.

The state made its case simply: the crime was terrible, I was violent, and some pseudo-science doctor believed that I'd pose a future danger to society. Dr. Quijano made the same arguments about me that he would go on to later make about Duane Buck, another black man condemned to death row. Buck's execution was stayed in 2011 after the Supreme Court took issue with Quijano's claims that Buck was more likely to be dangerous because of his race. Quijano made similar claims about Latino defendants as well, contributing to their landing on death row.

My attorney and my family were climbing a steep slope, trying to chip away at the inhumanity the state built into its case. It fell on the shoulders of my family to convince strangers that I was worth saving. Their heartbreak over the verdict couldn't last long. They couldn't wallow in grief. They had to talk about my smile, my sense of humor, and how I once jumped for joy after hitting a go-ahead home run in Little League baseball. Anything to help the jury see that I was human.

My sister Demetria took the stand first. She told the court about the months I spent living with her and her husband in Austin. I would go to work, she said, and come home to help care for her children while she and her husband were at night school, trying to grind out a little opportunity for their family. As she spoke, I recalled helping my seven-year-old nephew with his homework. She talked about his struggles with reading and writing, and how I helped him work through the challenging words that second-graders might otherwise just skip over. I wasn't an expert. Far from it, really. But, as she told the court, I did my best to make sure her two-month-old daughter had the food she needed. It must have been a challenging view-point for the jury members. They'd convicted me of killing children around those same ages. They must have wondered what changed in me between the time I cared for these kids and the time the state said I killed the others. I wanted to tell them that nothing had changed between those long-ago nights with my family and the night when the Davises were murdered in their house. I was the same, and I was never a murderer.

My fourteen-year-old son Terrell was next to testify. He'd been afflicted with sickle-cell anemia since the age of two. I used to sleep next to him in the hospital room when he needed a blood transfusion. As I watched him walk toward the stand, I remembered how scared I was for him when he was young, how we weren't sure whether he'd make it. He offered simple testimony.

"My dad is always there for me. I need him, especially when I'm sick." My son was begging a group of strangers to spare my life. I would have done anything to protect him from that moment, from the pain it clearly caused him. And here he was, trying in vain to protect me. I couldn't keep myself from sobbing, but the tears came without the faintest hint of relief. They were tears that had built up in my heart over two years of grief. I'd kept them in, knowing I needed to be strong for my lawyers and for my family, but now the tears poured out in public and all could see my despair. My son was pleading for the jury to see me not as a criminal but as a man, as a father.

His was the last testimony. The jury took his words and those of all the others back to the same room where they had decided that I was guilty of capital murder. Their time behind that closed door was shorter than it had been before. They took just more than an hour to make their decision. They returned to the courtroom with the same pomp and circumstance that they'd invited during the first phase of the trial. The jury foreman again handed the judge a piece of paper. The judge knew that whatever the note said would stir emotions in the court. His directions didn't present much cause for optimism.

"After I read this verdict, I don't want any unruly behavior. Respect this court."

I'm not even sure I heard him talking. I certainly didn't fixate on his words as I had in the past. The scene was blurry. I rose to my feet on his command.

"The State of Texas now sentences Anthony Charles Graves to death by lethal injection."

I felt the heat of a hundred eyes on me. If they wondered how I would react, I couldn't. I stood there, still. It wasn't as much shock as it was emotional exhaustion. I was like a man who'd run a marathon only to get some life-altering bad news at the twenty-six-mile marker. I might have wanted to react. I just couldn't.

Sebesta took the chance to rub a little more salt in the gaping wound. "Judge, I don't think the defendant understood what's been said."

It was insulting. I knew exactly what had happened. I'm not sure what they were all expecting. Was I to scream at Sebesta that I was innocent, like I'd done a hundred times before? Did they want me to cry and grovel, demonstrating some guilt and remorse that wasn't there? The judge told us to approach the bench.

"Mr. Graves, the State of Texas has found you guilty of capital murder, and has sentenced you to death. Do you understand?"

I shrugged my shoulders in a sign of my resignation. For the first time, the fight had gone out of me.

Deep sighs and weeping from my corner cut through the court's uncomfortable silence. I turned to find my mother. I found her on the front row of the room's benches, sitting with my son. I was numb. If the human spirit comprises a thousand tiny points of light, flickering and burning for the good moments, the tentacles of a relentless monster had reached deep into my soul to extinguish them all. I was drained empty. An officer came to take me away. I shot a look to my mom. I mustered only a weak smile. I needed her to know that I was all right. I needed her to hold the hope that I'd momentarily lost. I felt like an athlete walking through the tunnel after a crushing defeat, not knowing if he could get the energy up for another game.

"It's not over yet," my brother said. "Keep your head up."

My family reminded me that it was only halftime.

I couldn't respond. I acknowledged them and kept walking, back to a different type of locker room.

"THE JUDGE"

He sentenced me to die,
As though he would live forever.
He looked me in the eye,
I thought I saw the devil.
He asked if I had anything to say,
As though he would listen to me.
"Yes, your honor, I didn't do this!"
"Not now, Son, there's no need."
He said, "Take him away.
Put him in his cell,
Until we put that needle in his arm,
And send him to hell."
"Good luck, Son,
And may God have mercy on your soul.
In case you didn't do it,
You'll get out when you are old."
"Hold your head up,
Son," I heard my mother say.
Just keep saying your prayers,
Because God is the way.
"Bye Daddy," my son said.
"I love you, Daddy."
Tears came to my eyes,
I lowered my head.
Stay strong and hold on,
The rest of my family cried,
You're going to be free
Because the state has lied.
I haven't seen his Honor
Since he sentenced me to death.
I wonder if he's still living,
Or has he taken his last breath?
—Anthony Graves
  from Texas Death Row, 2004

I wrote that poem ten years after my sentencing. It took me a long time to process that difficult day. After a decade, I finally put my view of the day into words, as a way to better understand what had happened to me. Nothing happens quickly in the system, even after a death sentence. I didn't immediately go to death row. Rather, officers took me back to the jail where I'd spent the last few weeks. One thing was different: they kept me away from other inmates. I worried about my family. How did they take it? Was my mom still standing? A fellow inmate approached the door of my single cell.

"Hey, Graves?" he said. "Man, what, uh, happened in there?" I didn't know whether the news had trickled back into the jail or whether he could tell from my body language. Maybe he just knew what I knew when they took me to court that morning, that the outcome was all but certain.

"They gave me the death penalty," I admitted for the first time. He had no response. What do you say to a man who's just been given the death penalty?

He just shook his head and let out a sigh. His body language said to me that he really felt for what I was going through, but didn't know me well enough to know how to offer any comfort. I was grappling with the reality of my sentencing, but I didn't want to wallow in self-pity. I had a family back home to worry about. I called my mom to bridge the emotional distance.

"Hey, Momma, you make it back home?" I'm not sure why I asked the question. Clearly she was home. I had called her home line and she picked it up. I guess I didn't know what to say. On the off-chance someone's published a self-help book for mother-son conversations, I doubt it includes a chapter on what to say after you receive a death sentence.

"Son! It's good to hear from you."

"How are you doing, Mom?"

"Don't you worry about me. How are you doing?" I guess I took too long to answer because she started again.

"I want you to know this crap is not over," she said. "Those bastards will burn in hell for what they've done to you!" Mom wanted to talk about the case. She told me that one of the case's alternate jurors—a person who sat with the jury during the trial but didn't get a final vote—approached her afterward to say that the state hadn't proved the case. Robert Carter's brother had stopped by, too, to tell my mom that he didn't know why his brother had lied, because Robert had told him that he would tell the truth. I wasn't convinced that any of that mattered, and besides, I wasn't in the mood for optimism. After you're sentenced to death, there's nothing less important than what might have been said but wasn't. It's the silent voices that hurt the most. I shifted gears quickly.

"Yeah, well, how are my boys, Momma?"

"They're fine, Anthony. Don't worry about that. We'll take care of them until you make it home. Just keep your head up and God will work things out."

Others wanted to talk too. Mom handed the phone to my cousin Felicia only after giving her instructions not to upset me. The sound of Felicia's voice broke my heart. It was an instant reminder that I could not be home to enjoy life with my family. I told her the same thing I told my mom—to please look out for my boys—and then I shrieked and began sobbing.

"Why would they do this to me? Why me?" I asked Felicia.

"Please don't cry, Anthony," she said, her own tears muddling her words. I heard my mom yell out to Felicia not to cry. Felicia responded that I had started crying first. It was just like one of the old family fights we had when we were kids. That thought hammered home all that I was missing.

Condemned prisoners in Texas are not treated like normal inmates. On the day after my sentencing, officers transported me back to Caldwell, where I stayed for two days. There were no phone calls. On the day the state moved me to death row, all of the phones in the inmates' cells were cut off. I wasn't sure why. The state claimed it was a security risk, but it seemed to me this was just another way they tried to keep a man down.

I had been transported from facility to facility so many times that I knew the drill. Officers would come to the door of my cell and bark some instructions. I'd be chained in various ways, and I'd move slowly with either the aggressive or passive help of an officer, depending, it seemed, on how those officers were feeling about their marriages or careers that morning. This time was a little different though. Three officers came to my door. In addition to handcuffs, they chained my legs with shackles. I tried to take some control over the situation, mentally at least. If this was going to be my life, I would find some way to live it, even if I couldn't shake the chains. The officers were physically transporting me to a new reality, and I knew my mind-set needed to strengthen and transform yet again, in order to survive the long appeals process. I had too much to live for.

But as a death row inmate, I really didn't know what to expect. How does one anticipate the arrival of doom?

Up until then, there was always something in front of me, procedurally, anyway, to distract me from the heaviness of my situation. Not anymore.

When I reached the death row facility, everything was still so surreal to me that I had no reaction or emotions upon arriving. I didn't want to be overwhelmed by it all, so I just observed it all with detachment, in a kind of Zen state for me, the kind that I imagine when I hear about meditation, although I don't actively practice it. I knew I was going to either be exonerated or murdered. That stark reality renewed focus and my resolve. I began to see self-pity as a form of defeat and I rejected it outright. Living on my own terms could in some small way serve as an act of defiance. I had a choice on how I'd define myself, even if the system had pegged me a murderer. I remember thinking that I am my sisters' and brothers' brother, my sons' father, my mother's son. I was a sports lover, a flirt, a laugher. I knew that my life was about to change, but my identity could not. The world would know the truth about me: that my name is Anthony Graves, and that I shall remain so until I take my last breath on this earth.

. . . . .

PART THREE

SURVIVING DEATH ROW

PRISON LIFE, by Anthony Graves

Sitting in this 6 x 9 cell
Living under conditions
Worse than hell—
Locked away from society,
Simply because a man lied on me.
Everyone says: stay positive
But it's a struggle everyday
These conditions discourage me,
The shit won't go away.
I'm not always in the best of moods
Especially when I see the bars,
I'd rather be lying on the beach,
Looking at the moon and the stars.
Convicted for a crime I didn't commit
Is a feeling I can't explain,
It's the kind of thing
That drives a man insane.
You're a strong man
Is what I often hear;
But man, I don't think people
Really understand my fear.
Sitting in the cell 23 hours a day,

Staring at the things that's making my body decay.
I just shake my head, when I sit here and think
How the hell did I end up here;
This place stinks.
Somebody! Anybody!
Get me out of this place!
I'm not an animal,
I'm part of the human race! . . .
Well, I guess I'll lie down and try to sleep,
Because I really haven't gotten any in a week.
Don't forget to tell your friends
About prison life
This place isn't for men,
Children or your wife.
So, I'll pray that you never get to see this place;
It's not a pretty sight,
It doesn't have a face—it's prison life.

EARLY NOVEMBER 1994:
ENTERING THE LION'S DEN

· · · · ·

I ARRIVED AT DEATH ROW on November 1, 1994, the same year director Frank Darabont turned Stephen King's novella *Rita Hayworth and Shawshank Redemption* into the now-classic movie about a wrongfully convicted banker and his wise black friend. A green stone tower at the entrance to the Ellis Unit prison looked a little like the structures that rose from the Maine dirt in that film. A white female guard stood atop the tower. A pistol holstered to her hip, she also held a rifle in her right hand. She looked to be in her fifties, and her Southern drawl told me she'd been plucked from a roster of job applicants who lived somewhere nearby.

"You're in the wrong place!" she hollered down from the tower to the officer that brought me to the gates. "You've got to run him over to the diagnostic unit. They'll process him there."

Processing took a few minutes. Agents of the state asked my name. They took down some information and scribbled a few indecipherable words onto paper. I did a lot of waiting. A few minutes later, we returned to the green tower with the female overseer. The officer who brought me there placed his gun and some paperwork into a plastic bucket attached to a rope. The woman in the tower pulled up the officer's supplies like a banker sucking a drive-through deposit through the magic transport tubes.

I closed my eyes to block the shining sun. The gate opened and three officers placed their hands on me. They let me walk at my own pace toward death row. I tried to take in the scene. It wasn't much to behold. Death row is intimidating. It's designed as a testament to the ultimate power of the state to kill and control its citizens. I knew what had happened at my trial, but I still wasn't quite sure how I ended up there.

Coming to death row is like stepping back in time a few hundred years. When slave traders transported men and women from Africa across the Middle Passage, they'd drop those slaves off in cities like Charleston. Four in ten African slaves passed through Charleston, where they were sold publicly, in the streets, until the city banned the practice in 1856. Thereafter, slave inspection and buying moved to the local slave mart. The slaves were stripped and weighed, their distinctive qualities noted for potential buyers. A light-skinned female slave would go for $50,000 or more in today's dollars. A slave with a skill like carpentry would also command a high price. The caretakers of death row learned from that legacy. I stepped inside a pen. I was strip-searched in case I'd managed to pick up a gun or knife on the ride over from my previous jail. I had become used to the strip searches. It was just a routine of humiliation that had run its course. If a man can stand there and watch me move my private parts around for him, then that's what I would do. My mind-set was to follow all the rules and keep it simple. Next, an officer handed me prison clothes, which consisted of a white jumper and a white pair of cloth slippers for my feet. I finally got a haircut. A shower would follow. Once sufficiently clean, I was ready for the short ride to Ellis One Unit. Named for a former Texas prison administrator, it housed the state's death row.

Like most Americans, I hadn't given much thought to death row before my arrest. The writer and anti–death penalty activist Sister Helen Prejean famously said that support for the death penalty is a mile wide but only an inch thick. She meant that the death penalty's many supporters rarely investigate the basis of their own beliefs. As I walked into Ellis One Unit, I didn't know what to think. People typically focus on the death part of a death sentence. What they don't tell you is that *life* on death row is a torture all its own. I had no idea that I'd be living in a six-by-nine-foot cage, or that I'd do my business in a steel toilet in plain view of male and female officers alike.

If the officers didn't enjoy making me take my clothes on and off, they surely acted like they did. It was a routine that quickly grew old. In a back room, officers helped me lose the clothes I'd worn for just a few minutes during the intake process. I got a new outfit. The shirt featured large stencil lettering on the back that read DR. Once I was freshly dressed, officers handcuffed me and led me down the long road to perdition. The prison buzzed with energy. At that time, death row wasn't set off in some distant facility. It was just another wing of a functional penitentiary. Inmates came and went. Some stood around. The officers that led me quickly seized control of these inmates.

"Turn around and look at the wall!" one officer yelled. The officers didn't want general-population inmates looking at me. I'd later learn it was for my own protection. Even inmates in prison have an opinion about those sentenced to death, one officer said.

You didn't have to guess when you'd crossed the line between the ordinary prison and the place where Texas placed the worst of the worst. At the end of a hallway that seemed to go on forever, a gate with an emblem spread the news, seeming almost proud with its pronouncement: TEXAS DEATH ROW. I was scared. Thoughts of my family flooded my mind. No place contrasts as hard with home as death row. When I crossed over that threshold, it was hard to believe I'd ever make it back. I thought of my children. I thought of my mom.

Death row has rules. A captain sitting behind a desk inside the gate peered at me over a stack of papers. He must have been trying to determine if I'd cause him problems or not. His expression never changed as he looked through my file. Finally, he reached for a handbook that sat amid the mess on his desk.

"Read this," he said. "All of it."

I thumbed through the first few pages as he explained the dos and don'ts of death row. I nodded because nodding was the only thing to do. He handed me a sheet of paper that included my housing assignment. I'd be living on Wing J-23. It all seemed the same to me, but as it turns out, death row has its share of troublemakers too. That's where they put me, right in the middle of known gang members and those who'd opted out of the prison's work program. The work program was an incentive for good behavior. We could become eligible to work as trusties around the officers. The prison also has a garment factory where, as part of the program, death row inmates were allowed to make and sew the officers' uniforms. You had to be there at least six months before becoming eligible for the program, so it was too early for me to opt in.

The captain explained our schedule. On the weekdays, we'd spend twenty-two hours alone in a small cage, only a few feet long and wide.

Weekends brought twenty-four hours of solitary confinement because many officers took the weekends off. To save money, the prison would simply reduce manpower and keep us in our cells all day Saturday and Sunday. We weren't worth the substitute guards' wages that would be required to move us to the rec yard and back.

As an officer led me to my wing, I asked him why I landed on J-23. "It's the only place we've got, Graves." Texas's death row was almost out of vacancy. Five hundred men were waiting for the State of Texas to kill them. My cage had an address of sorts: Tier 3, Cell 10. The cage doors had bars and wire. They seemed designed not only to keep me in but also to make it as hard as possible to see the television. Maybe it was just my part of the neighborhood, but the third tier in J-23 was far from quiet. I looked around at the sparse accommodations as my neighbors hollered. It reminded me of the jails that held me while I'd waited for trial. Every inmate had something to say, and most wanted to say it louder than the guy next to them. One guy wanted aspirin. Another screamed for an officer to bring him a sick-call request. A few whispered to the trusty, himself a general-population inmate, to bring them newspapers, magazines, food. The trusties often became couriers, moving items from cell to cell out of view of prison personnel.

My neighbors went to great lengths to devise any source of entertainment. Rivals bet on whatever sporting event happened to be on television. It wasn't just the outcome of the game either. They bet on every single play with whatever currency they'd bartered for. I remember thinking that they'd bet on two crippled cockroaches racing on crutches if ESPN was foolish enough to put it on television. Death row was alive with men doing whatever they could to stay sane.

The sound of my cell door slamming closed behind me cut through the surrounding noise. I backed up to the door and placed my hands through the bean slot, the horizontal opening that would later serve as a portal for daily meals. An officer removed the cuffs. I was at least free to roam my space. There were no windows in my cell; the little light that filtered in came from small windows out in the hall area, through which I could just see a pond in the distance. The cage was filthy. Wet toilet paper and trash covered the floor. It seemed that whoever had the room before me didn't know what toilet paper was for, because the toilet was smeared with feces. I tried not to think about who might have left the mess. My emotions were already all over the place. There were so many things I missed. I missed home, I missed my life, I missed having sex; it had been two and a half years since I'd had the company of a woman, and I longed for it. If this continued, my penis would be sharp as a needle or as dull as a cucumber; I wasn't sure which, but I didn't want to find out. But more than anything, I was sad and confused in between bouts of determination.

I had been given powdered soap and a rag. At least I had something to do. Cleaning that awful filth wasn't the sort of task I'd have signed up for in my previous life. But that cage was going to be home, and I'd have to make the best of it.

My tiny cell didn't take long to clean. I scrubbed the floor while the floor scrubbed my knees. After twenty minutes of this labor I'd worked up an appetite. An officer and trusty brought by my first meal on death row: chicken and dumplings. This homey dish combines meat, dough, and gravy in a charming little glop. The way death row served it up, the chicken must have been of advanced age and a long time dead before its guts went to make that meal. Something passing for juice accompanied the meal, offered in a plastic bucket. I later learned that the juice served many purposes on death row. Some inmates used it to clean the stains from their coffeepots.

I couldn't have been more than two bites in when I decided I'd rather go hungry that night. I walked to my cage door and slid the tray under it, passing my uneaten food to the porter, the trusted prisoner lucky enough to have been given the job of clearing my tray. It was his problem now.

I toyed for a minute with the thin blue mattress that sat atop my steel bed. It seemed like everything was steel. Not the mattress, though. It was the kind of plastic that would stick to your skin when the temperature rose. I lay down and put headphones over my ears. I was surprised that the officers had given me a pair of headphones since, after all, this was death row. When I first arrived here, we were able to watch television, and the headphones were given to us to plug into a portal in the wall that would allow me to hear the television from afar. Or I could turn the knob and listen to a radio station that had been preset. I think the headphones were a little thing that they could give, with a pretty big impact on the environment in there: it made it a lot quieter, and caused the guys to chill out rather than be at one another's throats all the time.

Music gave me some semblance of peace. I'd pull a blanket over my head. My fellow inmates might have thought I was scared. I was actually trying to escape the doom for a while, by blocking out the present, and thinking about exactly what I would be doing at home. Literally, I tried to live minute to minute in another place, rather than one second in this one. I spent most of those early days lying on my bunk with my headphones on, checked out. I thought that if I just resisted the environment, it might not feel so real. I didn't want to talk or make friends. The food offered no distraction. I remained mostly a mystery to the men who weren't immediately a cell door away from me. Who is this new guy? I heard them ask.

The following week, my mom came down to visit me. We were sitting in front of each other for the first time since I had been given the death penalty. We didn't really know what to say, so I took control of the conversation and let her know that I was OK. I needed to assure her that people weren't just back there trying to kill each other since this was the first time I did not have access to a phone to call her every day.

My first trip to the shower was better than I expected. A beautiful black woman approached my cage. "Are you ready to take a shower?" I was taken by her eyes. For a couple of years, the faces above the badges had been almost all white and male. She was different. Her hair wasn't fancy. Her demeanor suggested that it didn't need to be. It sat in a bun, revealing light brown skin and perfectly symmetrical collarbones. She was more relaxed than most guards, smiling more than the men who believed that intimidation was a part of their job description. I walked with her to the shower, wearing only white boxer shorts and socks, with my towel and soap dish in my hands, which were cinched behind my back.

A door separated the interior of the shower from a makeshift viewing area in the hall outside. Little other than mesh obscured the view. She sat on a trash can just beyond the door and didn't pretend to look the other way. It was a part of the deal down there. Privacy was not an option. I stood in a pair of white socks and nothing else, and the socks served as makeshift shower shoes to protect my toes from the fungus that surely lurked on the faux-tile floor.

As we walked from the shower back to the third tier, inmates catcalled her. They hollered whatever came to mind in the moment. All were in search of the same thing—a distraction from the tedium of our condemned condition. She turned to me, as if to explain why she hadn't responded to their nonsense.

"I am not going down there just so they can look at my ass."

I smiled.

"You can't hold it against them."

"Yeah, well, this is all day long," she replied.

The place didn't suit her. Back in my cell, I wondered how she got there, why she'd taken a job walking inmates from their cages to the showers.

I imagine this woman knew some of the things I was thinking about while looking at her, but she never acknowledged it. It was wishful thinking on my part that she would.

I later found out she wasn't as innocent as I thought. She was trafficking in all the ordinary contraband that took on greater value in prison. Inmates paid her hundreds of dollars to deliver cigarettes and weed. One guy even arranged for her to bring him $500 from a friend on the outside. She had taken the money for herself. Those sorts of deals could be dangerous even for female officers. Some of the men on death row were there specifically because they didn't discriminate in their crimes between men and women. Our trip to the shower was the last bit of meaningful time I spent with her. She transferred to another unit after a couple of weeks.

However, she got me thinking more about everything I was missing on the outside. I would often lie in my bunk at night listening to Majic 102.1, the radio station out of Houston. The DJ Rudy V, host of a program called *The Quiet Storm*, played all the old-school slow jams, like the O'Jays' "Stairway to Heaven" and Prince's "Scandalous." When that song came on, you would hear guys holler out to one another from their cells. Being with a woman was definitely on everyone's mind. I would lay there and imagine myself back at the little bar I used to go to and dance. I fantasized about the kind of life I wanted to live when I was free again. I envisioned having a wife and kids, and the great life we'd have together.

I had this one scene in my head that would replay itself over and over again. I would have a wife and daughter. I would be at the park playing basketball. My wife would pull up with my daughter, who in this particular fantasy was always about three. My daughter would see me and take off running toward the basketball court for me. I would stop and pick her up all sweaty while she would hug my neck. I used to think about my own sons and going to a game or them coming to talk to me about girls for the first time, and how I would respond. Now I was missing it all. I'd been kidnapped by the State of Texas.

EARLY NOVEMBER 1994:
SETTLING IN TO DEATH ROW

. . . . .

I KEPT TO MYSELF FOR THE FIRST WEEK. But even on death row, the burden's a little lighter when it's shared. I knew that I needed friends if I wanted to survive.

"Look out Three Row, Ten Cell," a voice called out.

"What's up?" I said, both surprised and a little worried. The voice was coming from a cell below mine on the second tier. Someone had recently busted out the TV in front of my cell, and I could see, in the broken glass of the screen, a shadowy reflection of his cell. He introduced himself as Andre. That was unusual; most of the other guys I'd later meet went by nicknames or initials. I met plenty of AJs, DWs, Chili Bricks, and Chi-Towns. I had grown suspicious of friendly prisoners in the lead-up to my trial. But death row was different. The state didn't have anything to gain. I wanted to trust Andre.

"Say, Graves, why don't you come out to the rec with us tomorrow?"

I had been turning down rec time in favor of plugging in my headphones. Andre seemed to be looking out for me. He knew that an hour outside the cage could push back against the creeping insanity that charged toward so many like a beach-seeking tidal wave. I told him I'd come. He kept talking.

"The trusty gonna bring you a bag down there later on," he said. *What the hell will they put in this bag?* I thought to myself. But death row inmates were a hospitable sort, I'd come to find. They had exclusive knowledge of the terror I'd be facing in those first few weeks. The inmates would often send bags to newcomers, a collective housewarming gift. It was a tradition the inmates there took seriously. I wouldn't have any money in my commissary account for a while, so I couldn't buy pens, paper, soap, stamps, and those damn shower shoes. When the trusty stopped by my cell an hour later, I was sure I'd find those items in the brown bag he held. I was wrong. The trusty had brought a book gifted my way from whichever inmate lived in 2 Row, 10 Cell. I didn't have to wait long to meet my generous benefactor.

"My name's Rudd!" he yelled up from the cell directly below. "They call me Young Lion. Check out that book and holler at me if you need anything."

Human beings are linked by subcategories of pain. Addicts of all kinds draw strength from support meetings where they share stories of the temptations of bottle and needle. Even fans of the Chicago Cubs shared an agonizing connection with baseball nuts in Boston until the Red Sox thwarted the curse. The death row inmates at Ellis One Unit were no different. They looked out for me in those early days because I was one of the few who could feel their pain.

I pulled the book from the bag and gave it a once-over. The pages were crinkled. The first page was stained. I glanced at the cover, which was in good shape considering the book had lived its own life in a cage. A beautiful black woman with a proud afro stared past me from the blood-red backdrop of the book's cover art. It was the autobiography of Angela Davis. During my early days on death row, it took me some time before I was able to really engross myself in the book, but I soon came to understand why Young Lion had sent it my way. "We know the road to freedom is stalked by death," she wrote. I wasn't quite sure if I found those words comforting or haunting, but I surely identified with them.

That Young Lion was a reader might have surprised many outside of death row. At the age of eighteen, he'd killed a man during the robbery of a seafood restaurant. He traded his life for the $800 that the restaurant owner had made peddling greasy shrimp to unsuspecting patrons. In prison, Young Lion developed a reputation for violence. It was like that on death row. The man sending a welcome gift one week might shank your neighbor the next.

I witnessed a lot of bad things in there. Stabbings, suicide, men going totally insane, a few killings. Some guys walked around like zombies because of the medication they were given to keep them calm. I saw scars on men's necks, arms, and chest, anywhere they could cut themselves in self-mutilation. Death row was a dangerous place, all day, every day. Something was always going down. There were drugs, sex, and money, just like anyplace else. And the hustle was real. Officers were bringing in weed, crack, pills, cash, cell phones, and food from their home kitchen tables, all for a few extra bucks, and maybe a little for the thrill of getting away with it.

Meanwhile, more female guards started showing up for work. Some were having sex with death row inmates, often in the exam room where mail was sorted before it was distributed to the cells. The inmates all knew who had scored, but it was not common knowledge among the officers, as they had a different code. Some were selling sex to inmates who could somehow come up with the money. I saw guys get into fights over female officers they both claimed to be dating. When I became a porter and could move around, I gained firsthand knowledge of this information, which corroborated most of the hall stories passed around between the guys.

Most of the men, though, had female pen pals from overseas they'd developed close relationships with. I'd never been too far outside Texas, much less outside the country, so I didn't understand why foreigners would want to write to me. As it turned out, there were pockets of people in various European countries who wanted to correspond with American death row inmates. Perhaps they viewed us as sociology experiments—trapped men in a monstrous system they sought to understand. Sometimes it went further. Men would fall in love with the words of their foreign friends. Some pen pals would visit death row from their home countries, making thousand-dollar treks to meet the inmates they'd been writing to. A handful even got married. Prisoners in Texas, it seemed, were more likely to find a friend in Europe, where the death penalty had fallen out of favor among the majority of western European countries, than in their own backyard, where most fellow citizens couldn't muster a care for the condemned.

Encouraged by another inmate, I started corresponding with my first pen friend, and ultimately I had more than a hundred. It all seemed odd to me at first, but I wasn't about to turn down any opportunity for human contact. Death row is a sick and unrelenting monotony. It's writing the same letters to the same people to pass the same treacherous time. A new voice on the other side of a letter was never unwelcome.

My pen pals were all great friends, but with some I became especially close. Isabelle Perin from France was my rock, my superwoman from across the pond. She became my best friend during the long years I endured, my lover in letters and my heart, and my angel in fighting for my life. She visited me at least four times a year and would stay at my mom's home for weeks at a time so that she could see me. Together we would create a foundation called Join Hands for Justice, which raised funds in support of my legal defense and global awareness about my case. Isabelle sent her own money to me, too, so I could afford stamps, envelopes, and personal hygiene products, thus raising my standard of living in an otherwise hellish existence. I watched this beautiful lady dedicate her life to helping me save mine. I loved her for what I thought love could be from behind bars, but I knew I never wanted to get married as a prisoner, and I never thought of her as my girlfriend while incarcerated. I didn't want to commit myself to someone who was more of my fantasy than my reality. I wanted to be free to choose someone I could get to know under normal circumstances. However, inmates were trying to survive the best way they could, and if that meant marrying someone who would be willing to take care of them and help fight for their lives, then let the wedding bells ring. I understood the benefits even as I decided not to pursue it.

I had another close pen pal, in Germany, who worked tirelessly to help save my life: Mrs. Marina Vorlander. She would also travel many miles twice a year to come see me. We had a unique relationship because she was married, but we became special to each other out of circumstance. She would do things over in Germany to help bring attention to my case.

Nick Bell from Switzerland was the first guy friend I became close with. He showed me the meaning of true friendship. He traveled over to see me only once, but when he did he also visited a really good appeals lawyer named Roy Greenwood at his house on a Sunday while he was watching football. That got Roy on my case, which was super valuable.

And then there were Lars and David Augusston, a son and dad who would travel every year to visit me. They became close friends too. Lars started helping raise awareness in Sweden about my case.

There were others from other countries that came into my life and became close friends as well. I was very fortunate to have such great support from around the world, and they—in addition to my family—were a big part of my strength and courage to wake up determined every day. With all my pen pals, our letters to one another were so full of life. We talked about the death penalty, relationships, sex, the needs of a woman versus the needs of a man, family, our own lives. I would ask Sarah, one of my friends in London, to wake up on a Saturday morning and spend the day with me. This meant that she would get up and walk around town taking pictures of Buckingham Palace, or whatever she would see that day with her eyes. She would then number all the pictures on the back, write a letter describing them all to me by numbers, where she was when she took it, what was going on around her and why she took that particular picture. I was learning to live life through the eyes of my friends. Death row is all solitary confinement unless you were fortunate enough to make the work program or you got a cellmate, which was rare. But thanks to my pen pals, I started traveling to other countries through their stories and pictures. Eventually my network would reach several different cities and countries around the world, with friends in Germany, France, Italy, Sweden, Switzerland, Norway, and London. My friends in Europe would become my extended family over all of those long hard years.

Also occupying my days was recreational time, which I quickly discovered was relief courted by danger. I was often stripped naked again, and my clothes were searched, which was standard practice for all inmates. Two officers escorted me to a small holding room that separated the hallway from the day room where inmates spent their hour. The staging area was set off from the day room by a locked door. I later learned that this was to protect handcuffed inmates from being attacked by uncuffed rivals. It all seemed like theatrics to me. If an inmate wanted badly enough to get after you, he'd find a way either there or in the day room.

During rec hour, guys found their own entertainment. Lively Scrabble games separated the hard-core readers from the guys who just pretended. The library would allow us to order books from a list, and a population trusty would walk onto our wing with the officer working the library. They would pick up the inmates' library lists, bring back the books the next day, and then within forty-eight hours you would have to return the book by the same process. There were some other diversions too. Chess seemed an unlikely pastime given the crowd, but the worn set in the rec room got its fair share of action. A small television played whatever sports game happened to be on. Some inmates inflicted savage beatings on the boxing bag that swung in the corner. An outdoor area gave the illusion of more freedom. If you didn't pay attention to the razor wire atop the chain-link fence, you might think the basketball court was pulled from the famous Rucker Park in Harlem. There was handball, too, but on that first day, I didn't care to play. I had been told that death row housed the worst of the worst, and even though I'd received an unexpected housewarming gift, I wasn't sure what to make of rec time. It seemed dangerous. The outdoor space offered more room to maneuver in case I needed it, however, and I wanted to give it a shot.

The outdoor rec yard was a fiction writer's dream. There, I found men who had honed their own unique coping strategies. It was there that I first met Granville Riddle, who occupied one of the cells next to mine. Riddle was a young white guy whose hippie sensibilities suggested that his crime might have been a weekend at Woodstock gone tragically wrong. He self-medicated with cold busters, often paying inmates and trusties to hoard extras from the infirmary. He claimed to take ninety at a time, just enough to knock him out until six in the evening, when *The Simpsons* came on television. He loved Homer. Riddle's cocktail of low-brow comedy and high-cost medication helped ease the pain of years spent on death row for the vicious murder of a man Riddle intended to rob.

"You ever think of breaking out of this place?" I asked him one night, mostly kidding, while talking from our cells.

"I tried that once, right after they arrested me," he said. His answer caught me off guard. "They caught me three days later. I had a rifle and everything."

We would often talk until I fell asleep. Then he would paint on his canvas all night and sleep during the day.

In another world, Riddle might have been the sort of industrious next-door neighbor who could help me mount my television. As it turned out, he was just the man in the cell next to mine, in one of the oddest places on earth. He said he'd look out for me.

The men on death row surprised me. As I grew more familiar with them and their stories, even the worst of Texas's death row didn't scare me so much. I'd arrived expecting to keep to myself, but the intolerable cruelty of solitary living drove me out of my shell. I decided to take a chance. The underappreciated harshness of a Texas winter made the rec yard less than hospitable. In my first weeks there, I walked around, shaking hands and learning more names. There's a misconception that all men in prison claim they're innocent. It's a convenient fiction that makes it easier for those on the outside to ignore the gnawing guilt that comes with knowing that some men actually are innocent. In truth, death row featured a handful of men willing to describe their crimes in grisly detail. But it also had a few like Tony Ford, who'd been convicted of capital murder in the slaying of two Hispanic people in a home invasion gone wrong. Tony was eighteen at the time of the crime, and he swore up and down that he didn't do it. I knew the feeling. We bonded over the discomfort of our aligned destinies. I was able to gain release eventually. Tony is still on death row. I hope one day the State of Texas will do right by him.

NOVEMBER 17, 1994:
RESISTANCE ON THE J-BLOCK

· · · · ·

DEATH ROW SEEKS TO REDUCE PEOPLE to the worst thing they've ever done. But relationships aren't built on conversations about a man's depravity. I had to consider each man anew, to understand the person beyond his crimes. Riddle was a test case in this regard. He loved to paint, though he wasn't great at it. He often ordered books on watercolor painting from the library. Like a prison yard Picasso, he'd stay up late at night, painting pictures for hours after the rest of us had gone to sleep. Sometimes he'd paint landscapes, creating his own national parks. It seemed as good an escape as any for a man trapped in a cage. This wasn't his first exposure to paint—he'd learned to use it long after it learned to use him.

"What's with this painting, man?" I asked him one night on the block.

"I just like it," he told me. "Used to be, I'd get high on paint with my girl. We'd sit out in the middle of a field and huff all night. It was my retreat from life on the streets."

Once, he said, the paint took hold and he dipped off planet Earth into the depths of a bad trip. Dogs chased him in his waking dream, and he ran so far he ended up in a tree. Those trips were routine for Riddle. He'd become addicted to drugs at a young age, succumbing to the uncertainty of his surroundings.

Riddle's story was typical. Lurking behind almost every heinous crime was a backstory seldom told. Children growing up in crack dens, exposed to violence and harsh living. Many were abandoned, forced to face the world alone. They'd sought shelter in gangs, starting criminal careers that ended in some gas station holdup, some home invasion, or maybe a drug deal gone bad in a park. Their backstories didn't make their victims less dead. But those stories did partly explain how once-normal kids ended up facing the final weeks before being strapped to the gurney.

I was three weeks into life on death row when a killing came calling. Over the course of my twelve years on death row, I'd eventually see the state kill more than 350 men. The first was Warren Bridge, known then as inmate number 668. Warren was white and tipped the scales at less than 140 pounds. He was only nineteen when he'd robbed a convenience store and killed the clerk. At thirty-two he'd exhausted his appeals and had an execution date looming. Warren's execution offered a chance to consider the death penalty not in its abstract form, but in the reality laid painfully bare in front of me. Platitudes retreated at the sight of what was actually happening there on that day. The state was preparing to kill a man.

I didn't know how I felt about the death penalty at the time. Most people don't give much thought to capital punishment, and prior to my time on death row, I was among that lot. I never had time to consider the death penalty in its general sense. The moral and economic hang-ups were discussions to be had by policymakers and lawyers. I knew only that I didn't support it in my case. Advocates suggest that the penalty of death is a deterrent to crime, but I can't imagine that Warren thought much about the gurney when he decided to rob that store. As they strapped him in and carried him away, he uttered his last words: "I'll see you." It was a painful reminder of the inadequacy of final statements for summarizing even the worst-lived human lives.

The soon-to-die were allowed inmate visitors in the hours before their execution. Over the years, a few men chose me as their visitor, based on relationships that I had developed during my time there. Maybe I was a good listener, because I never knew exactly what to say. It was a sort of rapid-fire hospice, counseling men in their last hours and just being a friend. I think my life experiences—having a child at an early age and not having a father figure in my life—had equipped me for this odd role as counselor-to-the-condemned. I was twenty-nine years old when I entered death row. What I soon realized was that I had a lot of younger guys around me that the state had sentenced to death. I was quickly thrust into the role of giving this sort of advice because so many of them had come down there and had never heard nor had ever engaged in a positive and constructive conversation. Their whole world had been negative. My experience of having to be the father figure to my siblings at a young age gave me some insight and confidence to take that role on. One man I met with oscillated between readiness and defiance in those final hours. I watched as he struggled with the reality of the day, knowing the precise moment he'd leave the earth. Some might say it was worse than cancer. Those with terminal illness have their own death sentence, but they can wake up each day pretending it's not their last. There was no such option for my friend, as I watched his last hours tick away.

"You can't control what they do to you," I told him. "You can only control you." Maybe I was talking to myself, offering a measly bit of self-assurance in the face of the unthinkable. When the jailers came to take him, his legs went weak and his body limp.

"They might kill me," he said. "But I'm not walking to my death." I'd never imagined that choosing not to walk could be an act of preserving humanity. Some men on death row give up their appeals. They're called the "volunteers," a misnomer that suggests they want to die. In truth, they just grow tired of fighting. Their minds retreat to some dark space where death seems better than another failed appeal. My friend wasn't a volunteer. He fought the unwinnable fight to the end, never signaling to the state that his death was anything other than forced.

If my life on the outside was an exercise in trying to live right, to stay as far as possible from the thought of prison that swallowed so many black men from my part of Texas, then life on the inside was anything but. I thought about prison and execution 24/7 now. On the inside, men were killed routinely, one after another. Familiarity breeds opinions. Camaraderie took the block in the days and hours before an execution. We'd join in moments of silence. Some inmates participated in hunger strikes, breaking only when the state carried out its execution or when the Supreme Court granted a stay.

I'd figured out that the one thing I could control on death row was my thoughts. They could tell me they'd kill me, but they couldn't make me believe it. I stayed alive by living in the present, in the moment. This mind-set was revealed to me through my experience of living in a small confined space in a system designed to control you. I started to realize that they weren't able to control my thoughts no matter what they did to me physically. And knowledge became wisdom. But the constant stream of executions challenged the strength of my convictions. As I watched the state kill all kinds of people—innocent, guilty, mentally incapacitated—I confronted in moments of weakness the possibility that I might be another number on the list. The state understood that the mind of a death row inmate was the only thing they couldn't control, so the state did everything in its power to compromise independent thinking. Executions were dramatic by design. The trauma of those moments was every bit as real.

Staying in control of my thoughts was easy in the rare moments when death row was unencumbered by chaos. Too often, though, something stirred the halls. Men on the row were stripped of power and influence, which made them crave it that much more. The greatest challenges came when death row descended into induced insanity. I had been there a month when my neighbor gave me a courtesy warning, passing down a note to me. Notes could be passed several different ways, and one was just as common as another. Some officers would deliver letters for you as long as it didn't contain any contraband. Trusties were also allowed to pass notes between inmates—they didn't care if it was OK with the officers; they just did it and no one stopped them. And then there was the fishing line. This was a sheet that had been shredded and knotted into a makeshift rope. I'd tie something on the end that had a little weight, such as an empty toothpaste tube. Then I would crush up some state-issued soap, put it in the empty tube and flatten the tube so that it could slide underneath the bottom of the cell door and down the run to another cell. The inmate to or from whom I was sending or retrieving a note would take his stick—a piece of rolled-up newspaper—and attach a dental flosser at the end to use as a hook. Once my line was in front of his cell he would slide out his stick and hook my line with the dental flosser and pull it into his cell, and retrieve the message or attach one to my line. Then I would reel my line back into my cell. We all got pretty good at these methods. We had time on our hands, and we were desperate for communication, any form of contact really.

One night, a few weeks after my arrival, I received a note that read in big bold letters: *IT'S GOING DOWN IN THE MORNING, PICK UP EVERYTHING OFF YOUR FLOOR.* I was still relatively new, so I didn't know what to make of it. I turned to Riddle in the next cell.

"I don't quite understand, Riddle," I said. "What's this all about?"

"Just what it says, my man," he said. "Pick up everything from the floor because they're flooding the runs in the morning."

"Why would they do that?"

"These asshole officers won't let the porters pass anything between us. If the porters won't work for us, then we don't want them down here. We'll make the officers work."

Their logic was surprisingly sound. The men on death row controlled only their flow of water, and their toolbox consisted of little more than the sorts of fabrics that might stop drains from working properly. Yet this gave the men the ability to create a mess. On death row, this qualified as leverage.

It was all exciting to me. The daily grind of the place inspired madness, and without a break, you could drift into aimlessness, or worse, despair. These men confirmed my suspicion that even condemned men need a purpose and something to work toward. I lay down in my bed to wonder how I got there. It didn't feel real to me.

The next morning the 7 a.m. wake-up came shrieking. *IT'S GOING DOWN! IT'S GOING DOWN!* Guys at the end of each row had stopped up their toilets. Water raced down the runs, turning my cell into one of the steerage rooms aboard the *Titanic*. Water cascaded over the runs, pounding down onto the main floor below. Officers screamed too. Less than a minute passed before the officers themselves flooded the area. As officers worked to stop the flow of water, inmates shouted their demands.

"Get some rank up here!" one man yelled.

"Get us the warden!" another said.

"Get the damn porters off the wing!" a third called out.

Inmates leveled threats at the population porters who had come with the officers to clean up the mess. These inmates were sly. They knew that once they threatened the porters, officers couldn't send those men to death row anymore. The officers would have to clean the whole mess themselves. Chaos ensued. One inmate started a fire, with smoke billowing out into the run. Others broke their windows to get some fresh air, presumably to mitigate the effects of the smoke. I heard busting televisions. I watched as men threw urine and feces on the guards walking the row. Officers tried to quell the madness by removing men from their cells. They moved unruly inmates to "management" cells, the media-friendly euphemism used to describe solitary confinement within the prison itself. Officers donned riot gear to take on the less cooperative inmates. As I observed all this chaos through the steel bar and wire-laden front of my cell, I heard the screams as officers beat the men before removing them.

"Stop resisting, inmate!" I heard an officer yell. He wanted the cameras to pick up the sound, even as the inmate in his care took the beating without incident. The abuse was reciprocal in other instances. Young Lion yelled out to me, asking me to watch him through the reflection in the broken television just down from my cell door. He agitated and provoked the officers. I wondered what might ensue in light of the heightened tensions.

"Look out, bitch-ass officer!" he yelled. The officer failed to heed the warning. As he approached the cell, Young Lion unleashed a vicious urine attack. A nebulous yellow projectile flew from its cup right onto the lapel of the officer. Young Lion wasn't done. He challenged officers to open the doors, to come and get him. Six officers approached his cell door, only to find him greased down like an unruly hog with whatever Vaseline he'd managed to compile from shipments. Young Lion had dumped Vaseline on the floor, too, and used his T-shirt to create a makeshift lock on the door. The officers commanded Young Lion to back up against the bars. He refused time and again. Finally, they busted through his lock and prepared to inflict damage. Young Lion got a jump on them. Before the officers knew what hit them, he charged toward them, pushing an officer and sending them tumbling on the newly greased floor. Young Lion was ahead for what seemed like a few seconds. He climbed on top of an officer and wailed away, landing punch after punch to the officer's head. Then something changed. The six men found their feet and overwhelmed him. Where he'd been shouting his strength to anyone who would listen moments earlier, Young Lion was suddenly screaming out in pain.

"OK, OK, you got me!" he yelled. The officers tied him like a pretzel, his hands and feet bound together. They moved him from his cell on a gurney. I was little more than a spectator to it all. I didn't know what to think of Young Lion's spectacle. I had just gotten to death row, so it all seemed exciting to me. I felt like it was a scene right out of a movie. I understood right then how he earned his nickname. I had my own concerns—questions about my case, and the like—but they took a backseat on days like that one.

In Houston, when the floods come, low-lying areas are submerged with sand, trash, and crawly critters, leaving behind a trail of destruction. In the wake of our flood, death row looked a little like those rain-wrecked Houston lowlands. The guards cut off the water and electricity. Wet trash floated along the runs, bringing rank smells. The toilets wouldn't flush, and we couldn't wash our hands. The officers allowed inmates ten minutes each day for running water, but we got no advance notice on when those minutes would come. If you were asleep, you missed out.

We had paid a heavy price for our protest. But it seemed necessary. Flooding the runs was the last refuge of men who had their human connection threatened. Stuck on death row for twenty-two hours each day, men communicated through the books and notes they'd pass. The general population porters and trusties had helped with my initiation in that place, passing to me the care packages fellow inmates sent. Without that, men feared they might go crazy, and they were probably right. I watched young and old men lose their minds in the tedium of solitary living. Even though men were punished for their role in the flooding, and all of us had to live in the prison equivalent of a Houston sewage pond, the consequences were nothing compared to the effects of the manufactured loneliness the men had protested.

Protests require patience. It took ten days of mounting trash and official inaction for things to return to normal. I'd been away for a few days, transported back to Angleton to go through the charade of a motion for a new trial. Calvin and Lydia had filed it to help with my appeal, but like most motions for new trials, it never got off the ground. I returned to death row after a week, and little had changed. After a while, the captain agreed to let the porters pass items from inmate to inmate. No longer did the prison employ general-population inmates for this job; from then on, death row inmates served as trusties. Soon, new faces joined us on J-23, most with the same old backstories I'd heard before. All had killed someone—the death penalty is only applied to those convicted of murder—and most had done it not long after their eighteenth birthdays.

SPRING 1995:
ENEMIES AND ALLIANCES

· · · · ·

DEATH ROW NECESSITATED ALLIANCES. Many of the new faces moving to J-23 were friends with one another. Some requested a move to our
block at least in part to excise a feud with Young Lion. He had his own
supporters, and I knew it wouldn't be long before a vicious fight broke out.

From my cell on the third tier of the block, I could see into the rec yard.
Most of the time, this meant watching the basketball and handball games
that helped to pass the time on the row. But the rec yard was also where enemies would face off over whatever trivialities had arisen between them. I
watched television through the bars of my cell, a habit that helped me connect in some way to the normal life on the outside. From the corner of my
eye, I saw Young Lion playing a game of pickup basketball against Michael
Lockhart, one of the new enemies who'd moved to J-23. A hook shot here, a
crossover dribble there, and within five minutes, they were fighting. Lockhart got the better of Young Lion, throwing punches and taking Young
Lion to the ground. As the fight ensued, allies on both sides squared off,
not really to fight among themselves, but to make sure no one stepped in to
stop the beating Lockhart was giving. I watched in amazement, wondering
how it would all end. If no one was going to stop the fight, would they just
duel it out to the death?

I got my answer a few minutes later when officers busted into the rec
yard screaming instructions for them to get down. The officers donned riot
gear. They meant business. The inmates in the yard lay facedown on the
concrete. The officers slapped handcuffs on them. As the officers escorted
Young Lion from the rec yard, they walked him by Maurice Andrews, a

massive man who didn't care for Young Lion's antics. Young Lion pulled away from the officers just long enough to kick Maurice in the head. Young Lion went to the jail inside the jail. I knew it wasn't the end, though. Word trickled down through the cells that war had been declared. It wouldn't be safe to stand idly in the rec yard for the next few weeks.

Jermar Arnold, a close ally of Young Lion, was the prototypical death row inmate that legislators consider when they pass harsh laws. He stood taller than six feet and must have weighed 260 pounds. He'd cut his body with shaving razors. He routinely attempted violence on guards and inmates alike. Once, when I found myself trapped in a conversation with him, Jermar spoke of the time he killed a man in a California prison. Jermar had cut the man up, and worse, he tried to peel the victim's skin from his body. He was as sick as he was smart. When he wasn't intimidating those around him, he'd read for hours on end, keeping up with the latest books and magazines. The guards knew this and used it as leverage. They could make Jermar cry like a child if they threatened to take his books away.

One day not long after the fight, Jermar asked Maurice Andrews to come to the rec yard so they could talk out their differences. The courts had given Maurice a second life, sparing him from his execution with a last-minute stay. Maurice was so glad to have escaped the state danger that he forgot about the danger on the inside. The two men were walking along the basketball court eating ice cream. I could see them from my cell and I was watching them closely. All of a sudden, Jermar ripped a large screw from the concrete wall and drove it through Maurice's skull in an instant. Maurice was dead. Jermar grabbed Maurice's limp body and held it to the window for all to see. He screamed as he did it, "This is for you, Young Lion!" He slammed the dead body to the ground and stomped it, over and over and over.

It was the one time when the officers seemed like they didn't know what to do. They looked on, helpless and scared. For once, I felt some solidarity with the guards, and with the other men in our block. The danger was real. Before that moment, the politics of survival for me on death row had revolved around my case, and what I might do to prove my innocence. As I watched Jermar thrust a screw through Maurice's skull, I realized that survival was more immediate and pragmatic than I ever thought possible.

A welcome move to G-13 Wing in May 1995 kept things light. I'd spent six months among the so-called worst, and the constancy of danger had made death row even more difficult to endure. My move felt like most of the times the state had instructed me to pack my bags. There are no courtesy calls or bellhops in prison. In this case, an officer came with clear instructions written on a small white sheet of paper. My new destination gave me a chance at the work program, a now-defunct relic that allowed condemned prisoners to escape their cells for a few hours each day.

As I packed, I took account of the things I'd acquired in my six months on J-23. I'd saved up for an AM/FM radio and collected a handful of edible treasures. Roast beef and gravy or tuna felt like filet mignon in a place where water and bread is the wakeup fare. I smiled looking at the white shoes I'd worn to death row. The jailers hadn't done much for me, but they'd let me keep those shoes. They were a link to a world outside of that place. A trusty helped to move my bedding from my old home to the new cage. Something about G-13 was different though. Surely, it was the same hellscape that sent men to die. But it was calmer and cleaner. Women worked on that wing of the building. If J-23 was the projects, G-13 was a suburban enclave.

My move came just in time for the height of summer. The building had no air conditioning, and we boiled as the sun beat down on the roof and walls. It must have been 110 degrees and humid, the sort of air you wear. I've watched those reality television shows where bearded men test themselves against the elements. To stave off extreme heat or chilling cold, they come up with unique uses of their resources and surroundings. Men on death row were no different. I'd pour cold water onto the concrete floor, strip down to nothing, and lie naked on the floor. The heat overtook even that water, rendering futile my best-laid plans.

I resisted the slow dying on death row in whatever way I could. Relationships served as my lifeblood. They were easier to make on G-13, where inmates were less concerned with in-fighting. It's an odd thing making friends with death row inmates. I questioned what in my life had made me an illegitimate resident of the row, while many of the men occupied their cells for crimes they'd actually committed. Many of them grew up like me, playing baseball and working to make a life.

I soon became friends with Duck, a next-door neighbor who plotted to spread roast beef sandwiches along the row. He'd been on death row for two years. We'd talk about our commissary list like two housewives exchanging grocery coupons. I wanted meat, but I had a central concern.

"Duck, you think we can get some of that roast beef without gravy?"

"Where you think you're at, man?" he replied. "You ain't in that world anymore."

We talked for hours about the things we'd done in the free world. Like me, he'd grown up in the rural reaches of Texas, beyond the Houston streets that eventually claimed his freedom. His was a crime that lands many on death row. He set out to rob a store, not commit a heinous murder, but when a bystander interfered, Duck's gun went off in the subsequent struggle. We complained about the heat in our cages. We reached out to each other for mundane normalcy, to feel like we weren't dying the slow death. I felt some pride when Duck left his cell for the work program. It was one of the few times a man would move on death row to somewhere other than the death chamber. Eventually Duck's sentence was commuted to life in prison. I didn't want his fate; I wanted off death row and back to my home.

Five long months passed on G-13 before I got the call-up for the work program. I started out working in the garment factory sewing officers' uniforms, and then I got a trusty, or porter, job working on the pod. I would set up the food cart and help pass out the trays to the inmates in their cells. While they were eating, I would pick up all the clothes out of the showers. Then I'd collect all the trays and sweep up the wing. I felt like a janitor. I *was* a janitor. Prison officials use a host of carrots and sticks to motivate inmates, even on death row. Bad behavior is punished with beatings, or in a more official sense, with trips to even more restrictive solitary confinement. The system worked, for the most part. The camaraderie among the guys in the work program was totally different than the general population, even on death row. Guys had an incentive not to mess up. The less restrictive movement meant a lot to most guys. You did have some knuckleheads that snuck through the cracks, but they would only stay long enough to get in trouble and go back to the more restrictive setting. Guys on this wing played basketball all day. Some would be right next to the basketball court playing handball, or several guys would huddle over in a corner talking about the laws around the death penalty, or a particular issue coming up in their case. And then you had a few guys over in another corner smoking weed or shooting dice, always beyond the watchful eyes of guards, even though everyone knew full well what was going on. It was all part of the give-and-take we traded to cope and minimize violence. Overall, the vibe was totally different at G-13. Inmates and officers got a chance to get to know one another really well in that environment. One female officer came up pregnant. The institution was losing control. Every time they would shake down the cells, they would find weed, money, and crack. No matter how many times they raided, they would always find something. It had gotten so bad that when you were escorted off the wing to go to a visit or the doctor, the smell of weed would be so strong in the hallways the officers just started ignoring it for the most part. Death row had been taken over by the inmates through the guards. I felt better in this environment. But I didn't fool myself. I knew where I was. I still had no real freedom beyond my imagination.

NOVEMBER 1997:
THE NEW NORMAL—WORK, PLAY,
AND FAMILY ON DEATH ROW

. . . . .

IF YOU CONDUCTED A POLL asking the public to identify the men on death row with a handful of monikers, "father" would likely fall very low on the list. But most men there had children, and many of them kept on caring, even while disconnected from their families by the walls and the impending doom of an execution date. If staying clean and full felt like a challenge on death row, then staying a parent felt like a climb up Mount Everest.

I had to watch my sons grow up behind a Plexiglas window when my mother would bring them to visit me in prison, which occurred every three to four months. That was extremely hard on me. Before my arrest, I had been an everyday dad, not this. I would talk to them about what was going on in their lives, and give them my best fatherly advice. After every visit, I had to watch them walk away after putting their hand up to their hearts, and telling me that they loved me. I always made sure that I told them that I loved them when I could. But, as I watched them leave, I knew that it would be awhile before I saw them again. The next time they would have grown a little hair under their lips, then a little hair under their chins. They would eventually go through school without my being able to attend a parent/teacher meeting, or help them with their homework. I would eventually miss out on all their sporting events. I would miss out on seeing them having their first crush on a girl, and needing some advice. I knew I would miss out on the total experience of being able to be a dad to my children, and then they would become young men just like that. Men that I wouldn't get a chance to raise. Men I could only hope one day to get to know. They would become dads, too, as I became a pa-pa to their children, from behind those bars. Life would eventually move forward while I would always be stuck in the same year that I had been arrested. Nothing changed in prison, ever, while I knew so much was happening without me on the outside. So much I should have been there for, so much that was taken away from me and that I could never go back and experience.

My mother would often write to keep me informed with what was going on with the family. One evening I got a letter from her. I opened it, happy to be receiving mail for the day, until I read the contents of it. The letter started off with a greeting and then went on to explain that my oldest son Terrell had had a stroke but was doing better. She had waited until he was out of the woods before she wrote to tell me about his situation. The letter went on to state that he had to be life-flighted to the hospital in Houston. A nurse kept working with him as he was slipping away. He ended up comatose for two weeks in ICU. The doctors talked to my family about pulling the plug on him because he was showing no signs of progress. They decided to give it from that Saturday to Monday to see if he would show some signs of change. Sunday morning my son came out of his coma. I had to learn all of this in a letter that I read from my cell; I was not a part of it. I was a spectator to my own son's tragedy. It hurt.

I immediately asked an officer to let me make a phone call home to my mother. I told him about my mother's letter and what had happened with my son. He showed the letter to the major running my wing, and a few minutes later they brought me to the offices and allowed me to call her. My mom and I talked for a few minutes, and she reassured me that Terrell was doing much better. I was escorted back to my cell where I lay and fought back tears for not being able to be there for my oldest son. I had always been there for him. I eventually talked to my neighbor about my son and was able to get it off my chest. I just had to believe that he was going to be OK. I couldn't afford to start breaking down about every piece of bad news I received. I sunk very low that day.

It's every father's dream to see his kids grow strong, but dads can always remember the times when their children were frail and weak. My son had been through a lot. His sickle-cell condition made for some difficult days. Yet I'd watched him grow and thrive despite the health challenges. I'd kept strong through most of the legal hurdles thrown my way. I'd watched stone-faced as a court sentenced me to death for a crime I didn't commit. I'd even survived those first few days on death row, where loneliness and despair imprison men a second time. But when I learned that my son had been unconscious as a result of a stroke, I sobbed. It was a typical example of the pressures prison puts on families. Mom didn't want to upset me and worried about my emotional state. She'd kept the news from me until he was doing better. Maybe she was doing me a favor, but she had to play both sides against the middle. Perhaps she was right. I couldn't do anything for my son. Inside the walls of my cage, I was a helpless voyeur to the struggles of the child I cared for deeply.

The trauma at home drove me to work harder on my case. Death row can turn a man into a makeshift investigator and amateur lawyer in no time. I started researching the case law that was being cited in my appellate brief as well as the cases the state was using to keep me confined in this cage. I began writing letters to pen pal banks that had been established by different organizations asking for more pen friends to write. I wrote letters to the governor, to the president of the United States, and to the media. I created a nonprofit organization called Join Hands for Justice with my dear friend Isabelle Perin from France. The organization's mission was to bring people together around the world, in an effort to make one loud voice for justice on my behalf.

I'd been assigned a new attorney, Virgie Mouton, an appellate defender I hadn't met and someone, it turns out, I would never meet face-to-face in my life. She had worked as a briefing attorney with the First Court of Appeals in Houston and taught classes before heading to law school. In her letters to me, she struck me as prepared, but I wasn't sure how much that mattered. While defendants and lawyers work closely during trial, appellate lawyers work in the quiet recesses of their offices, removed from the person whose case is their focus. They type away, making complex arguments about procedure, almost as if their true client is the legal process itself, as much or more than the individual case motivating the appeal. Her ultimate goal was to save my life, and because I'd been sentenced to death, my appeal would go directly to the Court of Criminal Appeals, the top criminal appellate court in Texas.

It took almost two years for the decision to be rendered by the high court, which came in late 1997. After resets and delays, false hopes and despair, the court did what it almost always does in these cases. It poured me out, affirming the lower trial court's ruling. This set my case on a more difficult legal road, closing one of the few doors I'd had left.

One of the oddities of the death penalty system is that the courts run responsibility through many hands before finally killing the condemned. It's an excruciating process where hope waxes and wanes for the accused. I was in the early part of my appellate journey in 1997, and soon Virgie's efforts were buttressed by a newly minted writ lawyer named Pat McCann, who came on to lead the writ effort and inject new eyes and enthusiasm into my team. Pat was fresh out of law school and full of the sort of exuberance only found in those brand-new lawyers just getting started. He hadn't yet been crushed by the weight of disappointment and disillusionment that seeps into most appellate lawyers over time. In Texas, around 2 percent of direct appeals are granted, and habeas corpus writs are granted just as rarely. Habeas corpus is the most important step in the appeals process. This is the first and only appeal that allows evidence from outside the record to argue the claims. The Antiterrorism and Effective Death Penalty Act, which Bill Clinton signed into law in 1996 streamlined the appellate process so the inmate would only get "one bite of the apple." Once you have filed the habeas writ, it sets the stage for the rest of the process. The first time I met Pat, who was charged with preparing this all-important writ, I could tell he'd spent some time with my case file.

"I think we've got a real chance here," Pat told me, his investigator flanking him at the Ellis Unit. "No promises, but I might be able to get you out in about a year." I didn't know how to judge that statement. I wanted to believe it fully, of course, but how could I know whether this was just another false turn in an excruciating process that offered very few true promises?

That qualifies as high optimism for those who work on capital appeals. In a way, Pat's excitement was welcomed. I knew better, of course. I'd been poured out more times than I could count by jurors and jurists from Austin to Angleton. It struck me that nothing would be easy. But the fight can only be fought when there's hope powering the process. Pat helped me take the first steps in a journey that took far longer than the year he'd proposed. Still, I sensed that Pat wasn't ready to do it on his own. No one on the runs had heard of him. One of the curiosities of death row is that you sometimes take advice from people with names like Charlie Machete, inmates without much book sense but with more death penalty experience than a whole study group of third-year law students. Charlie didn't know Pat, and he suggested that I broaden my team. After all, Bill Clinton had just pushed through Congress the Antiterrorism and Effective Death Penalty Act amid a rise of public consciousness in the wake of the Oklahoma City bombings. The law purported to make the appeals process "more efficient and stream-lined." Those words sounded good to the public and policymakers, but for men on death row like me, they read more like justifications for removing the governor from Texas's already speedy death penalty machine. Before, there were multiple stages of appeal, including the writ, the appeals courts, and the governor's office. Now the new law cut out some of those options, and that was a scary new development in an already intimidating process. My state habeas appeal would be critically important for setting the tenor of my future defense.

Nick Bell, my first male pen pal, who had reached out to me with a letter on his own, had been watching my case from Switzerland, writing occasionally and helping to build international awareness. My growing net-work of European friends and allies were spreading the word around their countries by holding meetings, having fund-raisers, and writing to their own governments about my case. European media started to come over for interviews. European schoolkids started to write to me too; they'd ask a thousand questions about me and the death penalty, and then write a paper about it for class. Europe was learning about my case through this network of allies. Nick was visiting in 1997 when Pat joined my case, and, like Char-lie, he was convinced that I needed a broader legal team with more experi-ence. He sought out Roy Greenwood, a veteran capital defense lawyer who had an understanding of the process and the politics. Roy agreed to consult on my case, offering his assistance to Pat along the way as he filed my ha-beas corpus appeal in the spring of 1998. The working relationship was far from smooth. Attorneys have egos and different styles. Even those who mean well might not mesh together. On death row, I'd receive word that my team wasn't communicating well. In a time of quiet desperation, and with the odds already long, I needed teammates on the same page.

As the days crept by, a war was ravaging Eastern Europe. Pat, a US Navy reservist, got the call back to service near the end of 1999. He withdrew from my case right away, in order to trade one duty for another, leaving the ravaged masses at Ellis Unit for the battle-torn streets of Bosnia. His exit left Roy Greenwood free to take my case, and he did, becoming my attorney of record, and guiding the case through the appellate process for the long years that followed.

Throughout those years, I would get to know more and more about the inner workings of death row. In addition to my friends abroad, I began to make more friends in prison, throwing myself into the daily activities and board games with the other guys.

My reading habits picked up, too, because I now had access to more books. I would read anything from novels to the teachings of Siddha Yoga. I gained a thirst for knowledge, and I knew that books would be the way to quench it. I also started writing down events that were taking place in my life on the row. I wanted to make sure that if the state killed me for a crime I didn't commit, I would at least be able to leave my thoughts about it all behind me in my notes. I began to realize, too, that writing allowed me to vent and to escape my reality for a few hours at a time. So I would write every day, whether it was notes to myself about what was going on around me, or letters to my friends across the world. Death row was often quiet at night. Men would spend hours on their typewriters writing letters asking for someone to help save their lives. There was a little metal desk-top that stuck out of the wall right beside my bunk. We were allowed to keep our radio or hot pot on top of it. It was also our dinner table, as well as our desk to write letters or for reading. I started the book that you are holding in your hands at that table, where the words on these pages first flowed out of me and into my personal journal. I always tuned my radio to jazz music on Sunny 99.1 FM while I wrote. It was hard for me to get in a writing mode with music that had lyrics; I would end up singing along with the radio. Jazz allowed me to relax and just write as I listened clearly to my own thoughts, with the melodies serving as a gentle layer around me, in which I could enter my own little cocoon. Everything and anything that I would write in my journal or letters would be the truth. I wanted to make sure that if my journal and letters were stolen or confiscated by the officers for whatever reason, they would have the truth about my life in their possession. Everyone on death row had his own story to tell, so it was quite natural to be up late at night and hear other typewriters making the same zinging noises as my own. Most nights I was up reading or writing until they started serving breakfast at 3 a.m., and most of the time I passed on breakfast to continue doing what I was doing. Breakfast wasn't worth breaking a rhythm that could possibly help save my life, or at the very least, take my mind away from that awful place.

I also began paying attention to news about the criminal justice system. I became interested in politics and followed all the top stories of the day, as much as I could through the newspapers and radio. I started becoming more conscious of how the death penalty functioned within US society. The state had awakened a calling, a sense of advocacy that I didn't know had existed inside of me. I could no longer just wish to free myself from the nightmare that I was experiencing; my growing disdain for the prison system was igniting a new fire within my heart. I began to realize that I had to develop my voice regarding these daily indignities toward people, each one of them a human being, and each person suffering in ways I didn't think our society should allow. I witnessed and experienced inhumanity every day behind the prison walls, and I was motivated to become a change agent.

I eventually started working as a trusty on another wing, one that allowed inmates to be out of their cells all day. There, I could talk to the inmates assembled in the dayroom playing board games, watching TV, or playing sports. Marijuana was plentiful there. Most of the female officers usually worked the wings on the program, and that led to personal friendships and sometimes more. The line between inmates and officers had been crossed, and death row was alive.

I had logged three years on the work program when one night changed death row forever. It was November 1998, in the days approaching Thanksgiving. The holidays always bring a sort of insanity to bear. Some guys like to forget. Others dip deeper into their own personal dungeons. That year, seven men decided it was time to leave death row. I didn't know of the plans. I only learned of the great escape when an officer told me that seven men had gone missing, much to the consternation of the prison personnel and the surrounding community. I found out the next morning that the men had colored their clothes to fit in with their surroundings. They used cardboard to protect themselves from the harshness of razor wire that sat atop the prison fences. They scurried out as officers took notice. Those officers fired shots. Six of the seven lay down, content to live on death row a little longer. One kept running. Martin Gurule must have figured that he was going to die anyway, so why not take a chance? He ran right toward the small river that served as a boundary for the prison. Ten days later, the authorities found his body floating in the river. He'd been shot, and eventually drowned.

Things changed on death row after that day. The work program was suspended. Men were kept in their cages for more hours out of the day. The recreation program, which had allowed for basketball games, turned to something more sinister. All of a sudden, men were expected to fulfill their physical needs simply by walking around a small outdoor area. Even the artists took a hit. Because the escapees had used art supplies to obscure their clothing and scale the fences, death row became an art-supply-free zone.

The changes were in some ways a blessing and other ways a curse. I moved again, this time to a unit with mesh supporting the cage bars. I wasn't planning on escaping, but the mesh made it difficult to see the television. The near-constant headaches prompted me to watch less television and write more letters to my many loyal friends overseas. On the flip side, the move put me back into contact with Robert Carter, who had been living in a different wing of the prison since his sentencing. Suddenly, we were in the same rec group, forced to walk around in close proximity for the first time since he'd lied on me in court.

Our encounter was tense. Carter stood alone by a metal table. I walked up to him without a plan. Men had approached me before, asking if I wanted them to hurt Carter on my behalf. I didn't want that, and I wasn't after violence or some kind of revenge. Really, I had the unrelenting compulsion to figure out what had gone through his mind. Before I could speak, he began apologizing. He said that he'd always told the district attorney that I was innocent, but Sebesta had continued to threaten new charges against his wife, Cookie. He told me what I already knew: Charles Sebesta never wanted the truth. I had a choice to make. Bitterness is a heavy weight to bear, and on death row, I carried enough with me already. I forgave Carter then and there. We had been on death row for about four years together, but we'd never been around each other. I think I might have seen him in passing about twice since first arriving. When I was in Carter's presence, the strange thing is that I couldn't even be mad at him at this point. I had seen so much injustice in the system, that for me it had become more than about Robert Carter's lie. I was able to forgive Carter that day because I understood the games that Sebesta had played on him with his wife. Holding an indictment over her head with no evidence to support it was the D.A.'s tactical threat to make sure Carter maintained his lie about me.

Still, while I might have been forgiving, I was human. When I opened my mouth and started talking to Carter at that table, it took everything in me not to ask him if he in fact did the crime. I was scared to know, but I wondered how much of all of this was a lie. I didn't ask because I couldn't be in his presence that long to hold a conversation. I told Carter that the rec group wouldn't be big enough for the two of us. He needed to find another group.

Carter understood. He walked directly to the gate and told the officer there that his own lies had landed a fellow rec group member on death row for no good reason. I'm not sure what the officers thought I would do. Surely, after seeing men beat other men senseless for something like this or for no reason at all, they expected me to take out some anger on Carter. The officers removed him immediately. He was placed in a different wing of the row by the end of the day, and I never saw him again. The last time I had heard about him was when someone told me about the dying declaration he made on the gurney trying to right a wrong. Before taking his last breath, he was telling everyone who would listen that he had lied on me. I thought it was the least that he could do.

MARCH 2000:
MORE SECURITY AND LESS FREEDOM
ON TERRELL UNIT

· · · · ·

THE ATTEMPTED ESCAPE IN 1998 was the first time a death row inmate had successfully conquered the walls of a prison since a member of Bonnie and Clyde's gang did it in 1934. Naturally, the whole ordeal had legislators and local citizens alike on edge. We heard rumors for weeks that death row would be moved from Ellis to a more serious maximum-security prison. The early reports weren't flattering. Terrell Unit would be our future home. Men could expect less freedom, if that was even possible.

Officers didn't dare move every prisoner at once. They started by moving the men with poor disciplinary records. It took many months before they got around to the rest of us. The timing couldn't have been worse. I grew ill on the night before the move, and in typical death row fashion, there was no doctor to be found. My temperature rose well above 100 degrees as the nurse sent me away with nothing more than ibuprofen. It was precisely the sort of mood I didn't want to be in when officers came to execute the standard moving routine.

Ceremonial stripping precedes any move on the row. We were searched, then handed only a pair of boxers and some socks. Each man wore handcuffs and lined up single-file down the hallway. Inmates moved on a human conveyor belt, shuttled onto the back porch for further strip searches by correctional officers and Texas Rangers. I wondered whether my price was going up or down on the auction block every time I spread my cheeks, raised my feet, stuck out my tongue, or touched my toes.

The handcuffs were tight, as they always seemed to be. My feet were chained in such a way that I couldn't walk very easily. I hunched and lurched my way out in a kind of humiliating shuffle to the Bluebird bus that waited to take us the fifty miles to Livingston, Texas.

The scene on the bus was like the one in Forrest Gump. The seats were full, three men squeezed into spaces meant for one. My immediate seat-mate was Tony. I didn't know much about him, other than that he struggled a bit. The officers took advantage of him because his intellectual disability left him slow to respond to their many commands. Tony had to use the bathroom. He told the officers again and again. I watched as he squirmed in his seat, rocked back and forth, and practiced those tired methods of simply holding it. An officer told him he'd get to use the bathroom when we got to Livingston. Never mind that the bus had its own bathroom in the back. The officer was insistent that Tony wouldn't be standing up on that ride. I could tell he couldn't wait any longer.

"Tony, I understand," I told him. "You go ahead and do what you need to do."

I watched there as a nineteen-year-old man peed himself because an officer refused to take him to the bathroom twenty feet behind us. In another world, I might have intervened. But I was sick, and weak, and beaten down from my own time on death row. The best I could offer Tony was my understanding, the assurance that whatever he needed to do right then and there, he could do without my judgment or condemnation. The indignity of our collective experience was so great that any tiny momentary expression of individual dignity toward another prisoner took on a larger significance than the act itself. We all held on to these small moments, trying to piece together a way to feel human overall despite our awful daily plight.

The move to Terrell Unit (since renamed the Polunsky Unit, after its original namesake asked to remove his family name when it changed from a tightly secured unit for troubled youth into a death row facility) ushered in a new era of death row incarceration in Texas. Whereas previous units provided some semblance of vitality, Terrell Unit offered little more than a small space where men could choose whether they wanted to give up and die, or fight for life. For twenty-three hours every weekday, we stayed in our cages. On the weekends, we weren't let out at all. Long gone were the televisions, the basketball courts, and group recreation of any kind. We were crash-test dummies in a Texas-sized sociology experiment. How long can a man go without human contact before he breaks? Terrell Unit revealed that the answer to this question, like most, is that it all depends on the man.

Living in this new realm came with many changes, nearly all of them unwelcome adjustments. We began going on lockdown more often than I could count, based on some real, perceived, or manufactured threat or risk escalation. During lockdown, the entire death row unit was locked in their cells twenty-four hours a day. Prisoners were only allowed to shower three times a week, and most lockdowns would last between three weeks to a month. During this time we weren't given a hot meal. We ate food in a bag, or "Johnny sacks," which only contained a bologna sandwich, a peanut butter sandwich, and a small box of raisins. Most guys would refuse to eat their Johnny sacks and stick to the ramen noodles they purchased from commissary before lockdown.

Other privileges were taken away too, as a form of indirect punishment for the others' attempted escape and also so it could be made known to the public that things were under control on Texas's death row. For example, we were no longer able to exercise together as we once had done. Necessity breeds ingenuity, however, and we made adjustments to stay sane. We found ourselves working out in sync with our neighbors in the cells next door. I would hit on the wall, and my neighbor in the adjacent cell would start running in place with me for the next thirty minutes. We would then move to push-ups and sit-ups. All of this would start around 5 a.m., after breakfast was served, and became something to look forward to in an otherwise lonely day.

The harsh conditions were manifest in other ways at Terrell Unit, though we all continued to do our best to remain resilient. One of the creative things we worked out was a way to play chess while in isolation from one another. We would number our chessboards on one side, and use alphabetical letters that would run across the bottom of the board. If someone was playing for stamps (which we used instead of money), we had a referee keep up with the moves called out by the players. For example, if I were going to move a pawn to a particular spot, I would call out my chess piece, and then announce where I'd be moving it. "Pawn to Bravo Four" meant that my pawn should move to those coordinates on the board. Men played chess in this way over the run all day until nighttime. It worked because others would either be listening to the players play, or reading and writing at the time they were playing. Guys became really good at playing chess on death row.

Small privileges were eliminated along with the larger ones. No longer were we able to watch television, and we could no longer piddle (a form of craftwork using matchsticks, toothpicks, or similar objects) in our cells to help pass the day. Guys used to be able to purchase piddling supplies from outside vendors to make gifts such as jewelry boxes, picture frames, and beaded necklaces to send home to friends and family. No longer could we watch sports or play sports with one another. If there is one thing men in prison have in common, it's sports, and I didn't want us to lose that, so I started a fantasy football league in the unit. None of the guys had heard about it before, so here I was introducing fantasy football to death row. Once everyone understood the rules, it spread like wildfire. Every wing started a fantasy football league of its own, and for the next several months, guys would talk fantasy football nonstop. When we had our first draft as owners of our fantasy teams, there was pure excitement in the air. We'd go into the dayroom to start drafting our players to form our teams. Guys came out with their pens and paper along with notes on players and deals they would try to make. I remember when one guy, Oggie Doggie, who had been on death row for about eighteen years, came up to me all excited. He said to me, "Man, I haven't had this much fun since I was a little kid living in Germany!" He was a military kid. And then I thought to myself, if people only knew how important the little things are in life, they wouldn't take them for granted.

Apart from the ways we kept our communication, and friendships, alive at Terrell Unit, it had become a much lonelier place than Ellis ever was. But we could still have visitors. The first time my boys came to visit me there, I noticed just how far away a few inches can feel when there's a physical barrier between us. Like most, I came up with ways for showing my affection on visiting day. I'd move my hand from my heart to the glass, and my mother would do the same. A mother's love was one of the few forces able to break through the state's contrived obstacles. Visits on death row were permitted once per week for two hours, if your name was on the inmate's approved visitation list. We all held on closely to those appointed hours, as a way to stay in touch with the outside world, and also to maintain at least a threadbare emotional connection to family. The importance of human contact cannot be overstated, and now we had to substitute eye contact and Plexiglas in its stead. We did the best we could, but it wasn't easy.

Once again, I ramped up my letter writing in Terrell because there wasn't much else to do. Nick, Isabelle, Marina Vorlander, and my other friends from abroad would write me almost daily. I encouraged them to take their cameras wherever they went and share their days with me through their camera lenses. They walked around their towns taking pictures for me and would then write a letter describing each picture in detail. In this way, I could actually visit London, Paris, Sweden, and other cities through their photos and words. Their letters and occasional visits made me feel loved and supported by my European family.

Death row is a test of wills, a battle to see who can remain strong against a tidal wave of anxiety. Suicide attempts were up. The state seemed to celebrate the growing number of volunteers in this sickening category. One man hanged himself in his cage. Often, the run descended into late-night group-therapy sessions. Men would yell out familiar distress calls. I can't take it anymore, they'd say. I'd tell them that tomorrow would be better, even when tomorrow held only the promise of more of the same. Some cut themselves with whatever they could find. It's the sort of environment when you wouldn't have blamed a man for giving up. I knew I had to keep fighting, and more, to find my purpose before death row came to steal my mind. It was naive of me to continue believing that because I was innocent there was no way my life would end so unjustly. Naïveté saved my life, because had I actually thought every day for six thousand four hundred and sixty days straight that the state was going to kill me for something I didn't do, I would have lost my mind like so many others. I used to have moments where I would get tired of fighting, but I wouldn't allow myself to give up. I knew what the alternative would be. I would be executed for a crime I had absolutely no knowledge of and nothing to do with. I could not let that happen; I would not let that happen. I reminded myself every day with every fiber of my being, and I was just barely able to hang on.

APRIL 2000–FEBRUARY 2006:
EXECUTION DATES

· · · · ·

THE NEXT SIX YEARS were spent coping as best as I could, while men I knew on the row were killed year after year, sometimes with alarming efficiency. The officers at the Terrell Unit were going to be a challenge to get along with at first because they hadn't worked around us, so they didn't know us at all. They were told that we were all very dangerous and they had to be careful when walking by our cells on the runs. I heard one black female officer tell her white coworker whom she thought was walking too close say, "You know, they told us not to walk too close to their cells." I could only shake my head. She sounded totally brainwashed by a government system built to kill people. I knew then that this transition to the Terrell Unit was going to take some getting used to. As time went by, however, inmates and officers developed relationships that helped to de-escalate the tension and fear. Over time, the routine of living on death row at the Terrell Unit started to remind me of the same environment as Ellis One Unit. Officers began bringing in contraband, and flirting had started taking place between inmates and female officers. I learned that no matter what the circumstances are, men and women are attracted to one another, even in these surreal environs. Familiarity breeds not only contempt, as the saying goes, but also inevitable sexual tension between men and women.

The State of Texas was still executing people at a shocking rate despite controversies in many cases. Odell Barnes Jr. was executed in 2000, a few months after we made it to the Terrell Unit. An African American man from Wichita Falls, Texas, he had done construction work before coming to death row. He was born in 1968, and at twenty-three years old and with an eleventh-grade education, he had been sentenced to death. He'd been charged once before for robbery and placed on shock probation. And then in 1989, he was convicted of robbery and murder of a woman who was beaten with a lamp and rifle, stabbed in the neck, and shot in the head. Her naked body was found on her bed, where she had been sexually assaulted prior to her death. A .32 caliber handgun and an indeterminate amount of money were stolen from the home. It was said that Barnes was later observed trying to sell the gun to different people. The only thing was, Barnes said that he didn't do it. He claimed to have had a consensual sexual relationship with this woman. His case picked up some headlines in Europe. Attorneys started investigating and felt that they had done everything they could to prove his innocence, but the state wasn't going to listen. Odell Barnes Jr. was executed on March 1, 2000. His last words on the gurney were these:

> I'd like to send great love to all my family members, my supporters, and my attorneys. They have all supported me throughout this. I thank you for proving my innocence, although it has not been acknowledged by the courts. May you continue in the struggle, and may you change all that's being done here today and in the past. Life has not been good to me, but I believe that now after meeting so many people who supported me in this, that all things will come to an end and may this be the fruit of better judgments for the future. That's all I have to say.

And just like that, he was executed, with so many unanswered questions remaining in his case.

On May 31, 2000, the state executed the man whose lies had put me on death row. I didn't know how to feel about Robert Carter's execution. On the one hand, his lies had put my life in the hands of a state that believed in killing its citizens, despite the inherent room for error in this deadly machine. And here I was, an innocent man. The possibility that the same could happen to me suddenly got real in my world. Carter's execution made me think about my own mortality. I was in my cell the day he was killed by Texas. It was customary among the inmates that when an execution was taking place, everyone vowed to remain silent and refuse the meals from the state throughout the day, unless the inmate got a stay of execution and returned to death row. Everyone was silent the day of Carter's execution. I was in my cell thinking about what the state was about to do. I wasn't sad or happy about his situation. I was more reflective about the turn my life had taken because of Carter.

In 2001, it was more of the same. Jermar Arnold, who had stabbed Maurice on the rec yard, along with Young Lion, whom he had stabbed Maurice for, were both executed. Young Lion didn't go out without a fight. When the officers came to get him from his cell to take him over to be executed, he fought them with everything he had left. They had to pepper-spray him and hogtie him to take him away to his death. Death row was total insanity, it felt to me. Young Lion offered the following as his last statement:

> Okay. I guess I'll address the Morgan family. To Mrs. Morgan, the sister from the trial. Thirteen or fourteen years ago, I had a non-caring attitude at the time. I'm sorry for shooting your son down during that robbery. Politicians say that this brings closure. But my death doesn't bring your son back—it doesn't bring closure. I wish that I could do more, but I can't. I hope this brings you peace. Ursula, Mano, and Irene, I love y'all—take it easy. They've gotta do this thing. I'm still warm from the pepper gas. I love you. I'm ready to go. Call my mom and tell her that this particular process is over. Tell all the brothers to keep their heads up, eyes toward the sky.*

And with that, he was gone.

Texas had executed forty death row inmates the first year we got to the Terrell Unit, although it wasn't as bad as the previous three years, during which Texas set and broke its own execution records.† In 2001, the killing rate slowed down considerably. Texas executed only seventeen that year. It was still more than any other state, but by Texas standards, it was a slow year for killing.

But 2002 became a bloodbath of executions again, with thirty-six executions in total. This was the year Napoleon Beazley and Monte Delk were executed. They did not claim their innocence, but mitigating circumstances

---

* Texas Department of Criminal Justice website, Offender Information, Emerson Rudd #936, Last Statement, https://www.tdcj.state.tx.us/death_row/dr_info/ruddemerson last.html.

† Figures based on Texas Department of Criminal Justice.

should have resulted in a different outcome. Not all men are innocent, but not all men deserve to die.

In 2003, Texas executed twenty-four people, including my friend and neighbor from J-23, Granville Riddle.

In 2004, the state executed twenty-three people. One of them was a highly controversial case. Cameron Todd Willingham, a white man from Navarro County, was convicted in the death of his three young children in a house fire. He told the authorities that the fire started while he and the children were asleep. An investigation revealed that the fire was supposedly intentional, and Todd was arrested. He was only twenty-three years old, with a tenth-grade education. New forensic technology revealed years later that the fire was caused by faulty wiring in the house—it wasn't arson at all. Yet, on former governor Rick Perry's watch, the state still moved to execute Willingham, a sickening pursuit. On February 17, 2004, Todd made his last statement: "Yeah, the only statement I want to make is that I am an innocent man convicted of a crime I did not commit. I have been persecuted for twelve years for something I did not do. From God's dust I came and to God's dust I will return, so the earth shall become my throne. I gotta go, road dog. I love you Gabby." He issued a tirade of profanity and then took his last breath. Todd Willingham had been proven innocent, but it didn't matter to Texas.

I began to notice that most of the guys who were on death row when I arrived were now being executed. Some of them had become like family to me, and now they were being taken one by one: Dominique Green. James Allridge. Andrew Flores. Kia Johnson. The list goes on and on. I also noticed that the men coming to the row in those years were very young—many were between nineteen and twenty-two years old. This really bothered me, because I was meeting these young kids and they weren't the monsters that the media made them out to be. Most were kids from broken homes struggling to survive in a grown person's world, with odds stacked against them from the times of their birth. *How could we turn our backs on these kids?* I kept thinking.

In 2005, Texas executed nineteen men. This year also brought the execution of Frances Newton, an African American woman from Harris County. She had been an accountant with a twelfth-grade education. In 1987, she was accused and later convicted of killing her husband for insurance money, along with her son and daughter. She claimed her innocence, and many around the world believed her, but that had made no difference to the State of Texas and Governor Rick Perry. She was executed without giving a last statement.

There are many more stories of men, and some women, put to death in Texas during these years. Many of them I knew personally, but everyone there had some story to tell. Most we'll never hear. It's painful for me to wonder how many of them were innocent of the charges, like me, but had come to a very bad place through the circumstances of life. How many stories would go untold, how many lives were wasted? Death row claimed them all. When, I wondered, would it be my turn? It was becoming more real with each execution of one of my friends, each killing a stark reminder of where I was, and why I was there.

Meanwhile, throughout these years my case was wending its way along in the courts. They say justice deferred is justice denied. Well, I was in this for the long haul. My day would come—it had to. We turned over every stone, believing justice would arrive for me, however tardy. Along the way, my knowledge of the legal system and how it operated improved greatly. I had read so many legal briefs about the death penalty, and rulings from courts every day for several years by then, that I felt like an attorney discussing case law whenever the discussion turned to the merits.

In April 2000, the court had officially appointed Roy Greenwood and Jay Burnett as my counsels of record. During the same month, the state set an execution date for me. Roy filed a motion for a stay of execution, and it was granted in ten days. For those ten days, the proverbial gun was held directly to my head, but it didn't feel like a proverb. It was very real, and sickening. There was a certain date with my name on it, and in my head, all I could hear was a voice saying, *Anthony Graves, you have a date with death in Texas.* It moved from theory to fact, and back again. My case hadn't even made it out of state courts yet, and here was Texas attempting its first murder plot against me. After the stay was granted, Roy eventually filed my habeas corpus motion to the Court of Criminal Appeals.

In September 2002, my federal habeas motion was denied, and my petition was dismissed with prejudice against all the legal claims we'd put forth thus far. Roy explained to me that a ruling "with prejudice" meant that I couldn't raise these issues ever again before that court. Another door closed. One step closer to death. Roy filed a motion for a certificate of appealability on that ruling before federal district judge Samuel Kent, seeking to pry the door back open. We didn't hold our breath on this one, but when death is the prize, you fight every fight to hold the Reaper at bay.

Soon after the motion was filed, I had some unusual visitors to my cell. I was lying in my bunk reading a book, when two officers approached my cell door. "Graves," said one of the officers, "the major told us to come get you to bring you down to his office." I asked the officer why. I didn't deal with ranking officers too much, so I knew something was up. I always tried to stay out their way, because my fight was with the State of Texas, not some high school kid who happened to get a job as a prison guard on death row. The officer gave a nonresponse, "Let's go, Graves." And so I went through the whole strip-search routine to be moved from my cell, then put my clothes back on. I was asked to turn around backwards and put my hands through the slot to get handcuffed. The door rolled, and I stepped out to be escorted down to the major's office, which seemed like a long walk filled with uncertainty and apprehension. I was asked to take a seat opposite the major, who sat staring into my eyes.

"Mr. Graves, how are you?" he said, as I took note of his formality. "I'm fine, sir." The major got right to the gut punch. "The reason why I asked my officers to bring you down here today is because we just got a call from the state. They've set an execution date for you. I need to ask you a few questions. What would you like us to do with your body? And what kind of food would you like to eat for your last meal?" His words poured through me as if in slow motion. And that is the exact moment when I had a realization. I said to myself, *I am just going to live until I die.* It was that simple. *I am just going to live until I die.* They couldn't take that away from me, and that is what I could control of my destiny. As I look back on that moment, I recognize now how much those few minutes changed my life. I decided then that if the state was going to kill me, I would make damn sure that the whole world knew that Texas was executing an innocent man. By making this complete commitment to myself, I had turned a corner, and found my purpose. Only by helping myself could I be in a position to help others. I was energized by that experience, and I felt more in control than I had in years. Thus began my criminal justice advocacy in earnest, and it continues to this day through my foundation, and my approach to life.

Around this time, a former lawyer named Nicole Cásarez, along with her undergraduate students from the University of St. Thomas in Houston, began to contribute to my case on a regular basis. Nicole had become a journalism professor after leaving her corporate legal career behind, and this work suited her well. Her commitment and drive were much welcomed assets, and she even offered to write the elementary petition after we lost our appeal. Hailing from Canada, she is a mother of three children and a terrific wife, and she became an angel in my case, and my life. She kept hope alive through sheer determination, picking me up when I badly needed it.

In March 2003, we filed our next appeal, with the Fifth Circuit Court of Appeals. Offering the tiniest glimmer of hope, or at least a token symbol of success, in August of that year the Fifth Circuit remanded my case back to the lower court for a hearing on what's referred to in the courts as a "Brady violation" that had come to light. Withholding exculpatory evidence in such a way, known in the court system as "Brady material," is highly unethical, not to mention against all the evidentiary rules of our court system. To withhold evidence indicating a defendant may be not guilty in a criminal case is an egregious act of misconduct. When DA Sebesta went on Geraldo Rivera's television show and revealed that Carter *did* tell him I was innocent, although Sebesta said he didn't believe him based on a "gut feeling" that I was somehow involved, that opened a can of worms. My legal team dug deeper and was able to present a credible argument regarding the pattern of unethical behavior by the prosecutor, not just on one occasion but multiple times: Carter had told the DA, Ranger Coffman, and his own attorneys that I had nothing to do with the crime before trial, in addition to the grand jury testimony, and the DA knowingly withheld Carter's statements from my attorneys and me. An order for an evidentiary hearing on the matter was set for March 2004 to determine if the prosecution had indeed withheld evidence from me during the trial that was "material either to guilt or to punishment," thereby denying me due process.

This same month, Judge Kent denied my writ of habeas corpus. We asked for a reconsideration, and the case was referred to magistrate Judge John R. Froeschner. The hearing was granted and set for October 2004. Several motions had to be filed in the process. On October 22, 2004, Judge Froeschner denied all my claims. We requested time to file our objections, and the time was extended to January of 2005.

The final ruling against me came in February of 2005, signed against me again by Judge Samuel Kent. In March 2005, we filed yet another motion back to the Fifth Circuit for reconsideration, and this motion was granted.

It would be a full year before the Fifth Circuit made its decision.

. . . . .

PART FOUR

EXONERATION AND ACTIVISM

We must be prepared to accept the consequences of our actions for standing on truth, without ever giving up on infinite hope.

—ANTHONY GRAVES

MARCH 3, 2006:
SURPRISE FROM THE FIFTH CIRCUIT

· · · · ·

This next step is a trick step because it's not about innocence or guilt anymore. It's about violating one's Constitutional rights. We are hoping this court will grant us relief. If so, then we get the action we've been waiting on all this time. If not, then everything is still in the air. But I'm still optimistic and I know that GOD has his hands all over this situation.

—FROM A LETTER TO MY MOTHER DATED JANUARY 2, 2006, written from my cell on death row

ONE OF THE FEW THINGS that kept me energized during the long days on death row was baseball. One day in early March of 2006, I stretched out on my bunk and turned my radio dial until I picked up the faint sound of Milo Hamilton calling a Houston Astros game. When I was younger, I'd been good at baseball. Growing up, I thought I might be a baseball player, maybe even for the hometown Astros. Those dreams left as most dreams do for young men, once it became undeniable that Pony League talent doesn't mean a Big League future. It's not that these dreams die. Rather, the dreams of every would-be ballplayer are locked safely in a chest, accessed only through a day at the park or, if you're on death row, an afternoon spent listening to a game.

It was baseball that transported me from my cell and reminded me of who I'd been before my conviction. I couldn't control much about the death row experience. The state could chain my body, constrain my activities, and control my meals, but the jailers would have a hard time piercing the force field that protected my mind from the soul-crushing insanity of such bondage. On this day, the Astros were playing a spring training game against Cleveland. They posted eleven runs on the board, topping C.C. Sabathia in a game that didn't carry much weight in the baseball world but was still exciting to me, and it carried outsized meaning in what had become a somewhat meaningless existence.

It was right around the time that Eric Bruntlett drove in his fourth run that an officer disturbed my ballpark reverie.

"Graves, this is from another inmate," she said as she passed a note into my cage. "It's something about your case."

I left my bunk to retrieve the note.

"Congratulations my brother," it read. "You deserve it. I'll see you out there."

I looked at the words, stunned. They could only mean one thing: my case had been overturned in the Fifth Circuit, one of the most conservative courts in the country, if not *the* most. I usually joked that the Fifth Circuit was so rigid that Jesus could come down and testify on your behalf and there would still be a 2–1 vote to confirm your guilt. However, I would soon learn that the Fifth Circuit had ruled in my favor, 3–0, citing egregious prosecutorial misconduct. They overturned my conviction and ordered the lower courts to either retry me or release me in 180 days.

Roy Greenwood, the lead attorney on my case throughout this part of the appeals process, had not yet been in to deliver the news. As it happened, Nicole Cásarez, who had been assisting my attorneys for four years by this time and knew the case better than anyone else, had announced the ruling on a local prison radio show that guys on the row would listen to in order to get the latest legal news. As soon as she'd learned the Fifth Circuit's ruling, she'd headed to the radio station to tell the hosts what had happened, and they'd immediately given her time on the air to announce it in the hopes that I was listening to the show. However, I was listening to baseball at the time.

I stared at the words in the note written by my fellow inmate, the letters shifting in and out of focus. I wanted to scream with relief, but something made me hold back. Ninety-plus percent of the men on my block would get executed. No doubt my friends on the row would have been happy to hear the news, but my joy would have added to their pain. So I did the only thing I could do. I walked back to my bunk, lay down, and closed my eyes.

The tears came quickly. I pumped my fist in the air. "Yes!" I exclaimed. God is good. I said it over and over. The news spread quickly. My friends and neighbors at Polunsky (formerly Terrell) heard the good news on the radio too. But despite the happiness I felt in that moment, I had to keep my emotions in check. Keep everything in balance, I said to myself. If there was a single thing I learned while sitting on death row, it was the folly of sailing too high or tilting too low. Surely, I felt freer in that moment. The uncertainty melted away as my optimism was invigorated. But I looked up and saw the cell door still closed. They had put me on death row without a speck of legitimate evidence in the first place. What would stop them from finding a way to invalidate the court's ruling? Here on death row, I'd seen the worst-case scenarios play themselves out. A friend had received a reversal on his conviction, only to have a higher court restore his death sentence. They killed him not long after he got a note just like mine. The fight was far from over. So I remained guarded, even after receiving this extraordinary, almost dreamlike news.

The conservative Fifth Circuit's unanimous ruling was remarkable. Based on the judges' citation of egregious prosecutorial misconduct, my conviction was overturned, and they issued an edict to the trial court announcing the reversal.

The misconduct by the prosecution was varied and widespread, ranging from withholding exculpatory evidence and intimidating defense alibi witnesses off the stand to suborning perjury. This was all made worse by the fact that exculpatory evidence was withheld not only in a criminal trial but more specifically in a death penalty case, in which my life was on the line. Sebesta knew Carter said I had nothing to do with the murders and yet, the district attorney threatened to charge Yolanda, my best and most reliable alibi witness, with capital murder should she testify on my behalf. The DA had also knowingly allowed Robert Carter to testify falsely without correcting the record, or stopping it from happening in the first place. They allowed Ranger Coffman to testify falsely without correcting that incredible error either. The DA had also made false claims about another unsolved murder in an attempt to link me to it during a hearing with the judge, knowing full well that he had absolutely no "good faith" basis for making such outrageous claims.

The state now had 180 days, due to the Fifth Circuit's reversal, to make its next move. Either the state could try me again, or they could cut me loose.

Despite the huge win at the appellate court, I still had to return to the county that convicted me, because a lower court still has autonomy over its case, even after the higher court overturns the outcome.

Nothing happens quickly on death row. Five long months passed before anything of consequence occurred. The state bought itself some time by petitioning the United States Supreme Court to review the Fifth Circuit's ruling, and the Supreme Court took its time to announce that it would not consider the state's appeal. By September, the state had no choice but to act. I was finally going to leave death row.

An officer gave me a minute to say my good-byes, but I wasn't going home, of course. With the state planning to retry my case, I'd be moving from death row back to the Caldwell County Jail where I'd spent so much time waiting for the first trial. I packed my property and found some way to say good-bye to men I'd never see again.

Chino was my neighbor during those last days on death row. I rapped loudly on his wall in hopes that he'd come to the small slit between the cell door and the wall where inmates find a way to communicate. The doors were on rollers that left a gap between the door and the wall. I could go up to the door, and turn sideways so that I could peek through one eye and see half of my neighbor's face while we stood there talking. I knew I wouldn't be coming back, and I wanted to do what I could for him.

"Chino, is there anything in my cage that you want?" I asked. "I'll try to get an officer to pass it to you." It ended up like a makeshift garage sale. Among the gifts I left for my friends were the typewriter I'd used to communicate with people around the world, the stamps I would have affixed to letters to my mom, the radio that brought the Astros to my ear, and the money that filled my commissary account. I could have taken the property home, but I knew I didn't need it. Chino slid his line underneath my door and I began to tie on several items for him: ramen noodle soups, squeeze cheese, chili without beans, and other foods. All those things had kept me alive, and if I wasn't going to be there beside these inmates any longer, I hoped that my tools might help them find some solace.

I also called out to Ikei, whose real name was Anthony Pierce. He had been claiming his innocence for over thirty years! He spent all his time working on his case—writing letters and sending out packets of information in the hopes of getting someone's attention. So I decided to leave all my stamps with him. An officer agreed to take them to his cell. Ikei called out to me to say thank-you and to please tell anyone I could about his case. I assured him that I would. I knew Ikei felt very isolated. Most other inmates didn't want you to even mention their names!

Victories are rare on death row, and life is so scarcely enjoyed that an inmate's exit is cause for celebration. I was the twelfth man ever to be exonerated off the Texas death lineup. Two officers escorted me from my cell and put me through the typical rigors. The strip searches were nothing new, but the good-byes felt different. I saw men smile, as if they owned a piece of my impending triumph. I heard calls of "good luck." "Don't come back to this place," one voice yelled out. Pettiness had no place on death row. The capacity of inmates to care wasn't a zero-sum game. My exit inspired genuine glee rather than the jealousy one might expect.

The dress was different in county jail. From the white jumpsuit with DEATH ROW written across the shoulders, I changed into an old-school jail uniform with black and white stripes. The outfit made it seem like I'd been transported back in time, and truly, I was about to be transported back to the place where my journey began. I sat in the rear of a patrol car, waiting for the long ride to Burleson County. I thought first about the place I'd just left, and all that I'd seen. I thought about the men there, and how they'd challenged my view of humanity. The worst of the worst, or so I'd been told, but many of those men had become my friends. I thought of their stories and how I'd learned to control my thoughts in the face of excruciating cruelty.

I thought, too, of my family. I'd kept up communication with my mom through hundreds of letters. Some had been curt, a request for information. Some had been emotional, letting her in on the toll that death row took on me. I had high hopes that I'd be seeing her again soon. I thought about my sons, too, and what this would mean for their lives. Was it too late to be a dad to boys who had become young men since I'd been kidnapped by the state? Their lives had changed as well as mine, and I had no answers as to how we would go forward. It is not easy, after so many years apart, to just pick up from where you left off. My boys were now young men with responsibilities. They had children of their own.

On the drive to county jail, the sun burst from the clouds, shining through the patrol car's windshield in a way that only the September Texas sun can. It felt a bit like a movie, where after traveling many miles through the storm, the leading man finally makes his way to the other side.

I foolishly thought that my moment was right around the corner. But my return to county jail brought a new sense of isolation. Even though I was no longer on death row, I had lived on death row for many years, and I was the only inmate in county jail who had been charged with capital murder. So, the jail put into place new rules that applied only to me: I was put in a cell by myself. I was prohibited from spending rec time with other inmates. I had the visitation room to myself, too, and could entertain guests only after everyone else had kissed their families good-bye. The jailers put out the word on me, threatening trusties who dared to talk to me. Their classification system restricted anyone and everyone from being around me except the jailers in charge of their shifts. Visitation rules were severe. Twice a week I could have guests for twenty minutes at a time. Whether those guests came from down the road or from Europe, they could spend with me roughly the length of a commercial-free episode of *Seinfeld*. County jail surely didn't carry with it the constant stench of death's anticipation, but it carried other horrors. The solitary confinement suggested to me the state's sinister motives. They wouldn't be lying down on my case.

The food in county was a welcome change, however, from the inedible offerings of death row, where at times inmates served as guinea pigs for "nutritional" offerings not yet approved by the FDA. The prison guards didn't even know what they were feeding us half the time. There had even been a lawsuit to ban a soy substitute that had been found harmful to human health, a foul product that had been served up on death row for years.* Things were different in county. Friday brought a fish fry. It had been fourteen years since I'd had fish.

---

* *State Department of Criminal Justice v. VitaPro, Foods Inc.*, Supreme Court of Texas, decided December 9, 1999.

SEPTEMBER 2006:
UNCOVERING PROSECUTORIAL MISCONDUCT

. . . . .

ALMOST SIX MONTHS HAD PASSED since the Fifth Circuit appellate court ruled in my favor and sent the case back to the trial court. I continued to sit in the Burleson County Jail, waiting for what came next.

Now that my case had been overturned and set for retrial, I needed to find trial lawyers again, which meant that Roy had done his job. Roy was an appeals attorney who only represented clients after they lost their trial in the court below. He would then litigate through the appellate court process after the conviction in the trial court, and try to get the conviction thrown out and sent back for a new trial. Since we won our appeal, I now needed attorneys who were experts in the area of trial law for serious criminal cases. It was time to turn it over to some experienced trial lawyers this time around.

The first call went out to Dick DeGuerin, who'd left me at a time of need almost two decades before. We figured he might welcome an opportunity to make good. After all, he'd stated his belief in my innocence at the time he withdrew from the case. DeGuerin expressed interest but said he'd need a $100,000 budget for expenses. It was too much. Again. Before he made his offer, DeGuerin asked Nicole a question that still haunts me: he wanted to know if we had any celebrities on our side.

He wanted the publicity. We didn't have any. My case had attracted the attention of human rights activists around the world, but there weren't any Oprahs or Danny Glovers to ring the bell in the national media. So DeGuerin backed out and missed a second chance to fight my case.

Shortly after that, at an event she attended one evening, Nicole met Jeff Blackburn, one of the best capital litigators in the state, and mentioned my case to him. She was sure that Charles Sebesta and Burleson County were intent on a retrial, she explained to him, and that I was looking for representation. Jeff volunteered to take my case. Jeff's reputation was owing to a brilliant legal mind; he was also a slick talker. He brought with him David Mullin, another excellent attorney whose intellect was matched by a big heart.

Jeff and I also asked Nicole to become an official part of my legal team. She knew the case better than anyone, and would be able to help significantly if she had access to my legal records. It was the best decision we ever made. Nicole did her homework. She was diligent and persistent. She followed the evidence. God was making sure that I had an angel on the team. Together, the four of us began preparing for round two in my fight for freedom and justice, and for my life.

On the day of my first hearing, however, the judge on my case had other plans. There was not going to be any apology made to me that day. It had been a long time since I'd been in that court. While I sat on death row, Judge Harold Towslee, who had presided over my first trial, had retired. As is customary in small Texas towns, his family name never left the bench. The position was passed down, as if through some sort of hereditary osmosis, to his daughter, Reva, soon to be known as the honorable Judge Reva Towslee-Corbett. And you can bet she wasn't about to let her father's legacy get dragged through the mud if she could help it, as it might have been if my case was dropped. We settled in for a fight.

I found a bathroom where I could change into my free-world clothes. I wasn't sure they'd fit. For more than a decade, I'd been wearing loose-fitting prison garb. Tailored suits were foreign to me now. I wanted to look good, though. I'd learned enough about the justice system to know that the way one looks can shape the outcome before the trial even starts. Things shouldn't work like that, but they did. I had the jail nurse take my measurements so my attorneys could eventually get me a suit that fit for the many court appearances I knew I'd have. In the meantime, I slumped into the only suit I had, like a kid throwing on his dad's jacket for a one-time occasion. I knew I looked unkempt, but that suit beat the one I'd been wearing for so many years before.

As the hearing began, Nicole cut through my anxiety with a firm embrace. Jeff complimented me on my new look. When the clock struck half after nine, we walked into the courtroom hoping to hear some good news.

My mom sat in the corner with the rest of my family. I remembered the last time I'd seen her looking at me from that seat. She'd assured me with her eyes that everything was going to be all right. Now she had renewed hope. I gave my family a smile.

I sat beside Nicole at the defense table. Jeff and David exchanged pleasantries with the representatives from the DA's office. Their exchange gave me an uneasy feeling. I knew that defense attorneys needed to maintain relationships with prosecutors in order to get things done. But I didn't like the look of my attorneys smiling and laughing with the men who were trying to steal my freedom and my life. Nicole must have felt the same way. She didn't join the rest of the team at the DA's table. She sat beside me before finally trying to figure out just what the day would bring.

"Nicole, what's going on?" I asked.

"We're still not sure. The prosecutors said this is the judge's party. Even they don't know why we're here."

The familiar call from the bailiff shook the room a few minutes later. "All rise!" he said, compelling the room to its collective feet.

Judge Towslee-Corbett entered and took her place behind the large piece of wooden furniture designed to emphasize her authority. She seemed calm on the bench. As it turned out, the hearing didn't have much of a purpose at all. The judge wanted to give defense counsel and the prosecutor's office a chance to meet, and she said she needed to impose a gag order on the parties in the case. My lawyers didn't like it. For fourteen years, I'd been buried behind some set of bars or another, and I'd dreamed about having my day in court. That day had come, but the state didn't seem interested in righting its wrongs. In fact, the judge's order was designed to limit public exposure of my case. She didn't want the media covering what had happened. There was already an article in the *Houston Chronicle*, by a reporter named Harvey Rice, who had started writing about my case before I was released and continued to highlight the proceedings as they took place. He was put on pause by the gag order, but we fought it.

We eventually made a formal appeal. A district judge ruled that Judge Towslee-Corbett had overstepped her authority by issuing the gag order.

It would soon be lifted, but still, the meet-and-greet had an even more nefarious purpose. When the Fifth Circuit overturned my conviction, it mandated that the trial court must either try me or set me free within 180 days. The state argued that with the meet-and-greet, it had satisfied this mandate. The new trial had begun, prosecutors argued. This started a parade of resets. The state would reset my trial date for the next four years, finding some reason or another why we couldn't yet proceed. If the wheels of justice turn slowly, we were stuck in the maddening mud. My emotions ran the gamut as they played this game with my life. I knew that I had to stay patient. I knew the war of attrition the state was waging: confine you until you are ready to accept a plea bargain. I had made my mind up years before that the state and I only had two choices on the table to resolve this situation: they were going to have to kill me or set me free. I wasn't going to take any compromises.

Through my attorneys, the state offered a life sentence. I took that as a slap in the face. I knew by now they had a pretty good idea that I was innocent, and instead of acknowledging it and letting the system work, the new presiding judge decided that she would postpone the case as long as it took for her to find a way to retry me. I knew it was going to be a fight after I had witnessed the judge make one bad ruling after another to help give the prosecutor an advantage. By now I had my firm resolve: I was going to keep on fighting.

Many of the trial court's rulings seemed curious, and some were just too incredible to fathom. The Fifth Circuit had found Robert Carter's original trial testimony to be false. Still, the trial court judge granted the prosecutor's motion allowing that same testimony to be used in my pending retrial. How could any rational mind believe that to be possible? How could a trial judge allow perjured testimony to be admitted in a retrial for capital murder? Judge Towslee-Corbett seemed resolute in her desire to help the state get its second guilty verdict. I returned to jail with uncertainty abounding.

It was shocking to see how far the rules would bend toward the prosecution, and how accepted it was when it happened. I had a very hard time accepting it myself, and still cannot believe that Towslee-Corbett ignored the Fifth Circuit's opinion and allowed the prosecutors to use Robert Carter's perjured testimony a second time, even though a higher court had found the testimony to be a lie. My attorneys and I were always of the mind that, because she was presiding over a case in which her father had presided and got it wrong, she was unable to be impartial. We were right. She did everything she could do to give the prosecution an edge. She made one bad legal ruling after another.

We filed a new motion asking the judge to provide us with any information that might cause her to have to recuse herself. Instead of responding to the motion, she set up a recusal hearing without our knowledge. Towslee-Corbett brought in her district judge to preside over this hearing. When my attorneys told this judge that we hadn't been informed that this recusal hearing was granted or scheduled for that day, and that we weren't prepared to be heard on the matter, the district judge denied our argument and ruled that Judge Towslee-Corbett had every right to stay on the case. I wasn't shocked by this outcome, because I had seen this type of behavior by our courts for fourteen years at that point. I had witnessed politics playing a larger role than justice in our criminal justice system.

Nicole's visits back in county became much more frequent and personal after this. While death row put physical and emotional distance between clients and their visitors, county was more laid back. Officers let Nicole into the visitation area where inmates sat. There were no bars between us. We didn't have to make pretend handshakes through Plexiglas by holding our palms pressed up against the barrier. We communicated like friends.

She was my connection to the outside world, and over time, I became a bigger part of her world too. When Nicole first visited me and first took an interest in my case, we'd been very honest with each other. She didn't want to come visit me in the first few months. She was trying to review the case with an objective, journalist's eye. She feared that if she came to see me, she'd be wrapped in a bundle of emotions that might blind her to the truth. I appreciated Nicole's approach. By the time ten years had passed on death row, I wasn't in the market for any more friends. I just needed someone who had the ability, determination, and willingness to help.

"If you're going to come in here and help me," I told her during that first meeting, "you better be willing to commit to the long term." I'd had too many people come in and out of my case. They were tourists in my struggle, wanting to help but not really knowing how. Some had become overwhelmed by it all, unable to handle the emotional toll that came with helping an innocent man on death row. Many had good intentions but lacked the ability to follow through. By the time Nicole came along, I didn't have time for another well-intentioned interloper. I needed someone committed to the case. I gave her an ultimatum that helped to shape the future of our friendship.

"If you're not willing to see this thing through," I told her from behind the separating wall at death row, "then thank you for caring, but don't come back."

Nicole didn't say a word. She must have gone home to think about it, to think about the consequences of putting her family through the emotional roller coaster of a real innocence investigation. How would she tell her children if my case didn't turn out the way we wanted? How would she handle investing in the life of a man who might be killed by the state? Whatever the calculus had been, Nicole made her choice. She showed up at death row the next time for our visit. We never talked about that conversation, but when she made the long, hard drive back to see me again, I knew she had decided that the emotional toll was worth it. She'd decided that I was worth the risk.

As Nicole's visits grew more frequent, we developed a routine, and our friendship strengthened in the face of trauma and shared experiences. She'd start our sessions by listening to me complain about whatever had been happening in prison. The food served to us was beyond bad, the conditions were hot, and I struggled at times to hang on to the positive attitude that kept my mind alive. We'd eventually move on to the case. Nicole told me how she'd found information on the faulty loudspeakers in the county jail. She'd explain other ways my legal team had chipped away at the state's evidence.

In 2007, in Nicole's continuing work on the evidence to prepare for a retrial, she met with a former jailer named Wayne Meads. During my original trial in 1994, a man named John Robinson had falsely testified against me, stating that he and Meads had supposedly overheard me incriminating myself over the intercom speakers. Wayne later told Nicole that it never happened, and if it had, that would have been something he would have definitely remembered. His statement to Nicole was backed up by the fact that Sebesta never called him to testify to overhearing that conversation. Means died sometime around late 2008, after the meeting with Nicole.

Meanwhile, Nicole talked to Roy Allen, who told her how the DA's office had tried to convince him that they had collected all of this evidence against me. They claimed unflinchingly that they had my blood in evidence, and so on. They'd lied to him. Roy was especially upset with the prosecutor's investigator E. K. Murray. He told me many times that Murray and Bill Torrey, the second-chair prosecutor, were just as guilty as Charles Sebesta for wrongfully convicting me. Bill Torrey's name didn't often come up in the attention surrounding my case, but Roy felt he was in lockstep with Sebesta in the misconduct.

We discovered more and more incredible information, mostly through Nicole's work, as we prepared to challenge bad evidence and offer our own in anticipation of another trial. Despite having my conviction reversed, I was still at the mercy of the process. Would the DA acknowledge the many mistakes and dismiss my case? Unlikely, as that would mean taking responsibility and even admitting prosecutorial misconduct. That was never going to happen. So we had to scour existing evidence and chase down every claim in our efforts to be ready this time at trial, eyes open and fully armed with facts.

In addition to the false claims of inculpatory evidence, such as having my blood, and the souvenir knife that the prosecutors tried to link to the crime, there was a woman named Mildred Bracewell, who had worked at a local convenience store in Somerville the night the murders had occurred. She had identified me in that 1992 lineup as the man who had come into the store that night to buy gasoline. After my case was reversed, we arranged for Bracewell to attend a hearing, where it became evident that she'd had no clue who I was. She had given a physical description that completely ruled me out. And when I'd stood in front of her, she said that she didn't remember ever seeing me. She had just wanted to aid the police and ended up being taken advantage of, ultimately helping the state secure a wrongful conviction in a capital murder trial.

My attorneys had changed many times by now, so we did all we could to keep this information organized as the stack of errors piled high. Overall, I could sense the light switch go on for Nicole at some point in those visits, with all this information coming out and from getting to know me as a person. She started as a cautious believer in my case, and finished as a champion for justice. She was such an important part of my legal team. They all were at this point.

Often during my visits with Nicole, my conversations with her would meander from the case to more personal topics. I'd ask about her kids and how her students were doing at St. Thomas University. One Christmas, she brought me six shrimp in a plastic bag and a copy of the *Houston Chronicle*'s sports section. She knew it was the little things that prison can take from a man that sometimes mattered the most. We eventually moved to lighter things. Once I noticed her fidgeting through her purse. She'd forgotten to leave her iPod in the car. It was the first time I'd seen the new music device. She showed me how it worked, that fancy triangle spitting out whatever music you wanted to hear. I learned about playlists and the ability to move from song to song without having to adjust the tape. It was all "digital," which was a whole new world to me and illustrated how much was passing me by out there. "One thousand songs in your pocket" was Steve Job's revolutionary invention, and it was astounding to me to discover.

Nicole's playlists surprised me. I saw Michael Jackson and danced for a minute to the music. Nicole got worried, signaling for me to stop. Surely the jailers would come and crack down on us for making too much noise. I didn't care. Her music fed my soul. We'd eventually move on to sports and my obvious love of this topic. The Astros dominated our conversations during the moments when Nicole wasn't trying to slip in mentions of hockey. We were an odd team—the baseball-obsessed black man from rural Texas and the hockey-loving Canadian expatriate, trying to change the world from her perch in Houston. When the conversation moved to sports, Nicole knew she could go home. She knew I was all right, and that I'd be OK until our next meeting.

Our friendship wasn't one-sided, of course. For everything Nicole gave to me, I gave something back. On days when I wasn't as strong, she assured me of the work being done on the case. And as it goes, the work on the case sometimes left Nicole needing reassurance from me. I can imagine how hard it was. Just as I tried to stay positive behind the door of a prison cell, Nicole struggled with the reality that every caring criminal defense attorney must understand. In conversations since my release, I've talked to many dedicated people who've said that representing a genuinely innocent client can be a constant torment. It's those people they want to help the most, but the system sometimes makes it difficult.

"We're working as hard as we can, Anthony," she'd tell me. "But these people just won't give in." She seemed dedicated to seeing the case through. Still, some days she wasn't sure that the outcome would be the one we all hoped for.

Her doubt was natural. I dealt with it too, firmly believing that courage isn't defined by certainty but by the ability to face daily uncertainty with resolute purpose. I'd concluded that even if nothing else was in my control, I could control my identity. I decided to be the man fighting for justice, whether I died at the hands of the state or earned my release into the free world. It was that thought, and that comfort in this identity, that helped me power through those long nights that sometimes came after Nicole had no good news to share.

However, when the moment called for it, Nicole snapped from friend to fierce fighter. Back in April 2007, my legal team had asked the judge to remove Joan Scroggins, the assistant prosecutor who'd worked with Charles Sebesta on the original trial. The Fifth Circuit had found severe misconduct with the first team, and we thought the presence of Scroggins in the new trial violated all notions of justice. She'd sat on the prosecutor's team when I was first tried at the trial level. She must have had knowledge of all the misconduct that was going on in my case, and she did nothing to report it back then. It is every attorney's duty and responsibility to report to the state bar any acts of misconduct by another attorney. She supported Charles Sebesta's work, so to us, it seemed clear that she condoned his misconduct. We felt that her presence on the DA's team now would compromise the quality of justice the courts should be seeking.

This turned out to be a risky move. The judge didn't just recuse Scroggins; she recused the entire office because the lead prosecutor argued that she could not try the case without Scroggins. This set in motion the search for a special prosecutor. I sat in jail for more than two weeks on a capital murder case with no prosecutors representing the state against me. The judge decided to set a $1 million bond to keep me in jail, while she found a special prosecutor to fill this role.

It looked like justice in my case was going to be delayed yet again.

NOVEMBER 2008:
CLOSING IN ON THE STATE'S CASE

· · · · ·

WORD FINALLY CAME THAT the court had found a special prosecutor. Patrick Batchelor had earned notoriety in the case of Todd Willingham, a Texas man executed in 2004 on the basis of faulty arson evidence, what's now called "junk science." Willingham's claim of actual innocence had garnered international support, and his execution prompted outrage. Batchelor's appointment to my case didn't give much cause for celebration.

Lance Kutnick, a protégé of Sebesta, was tasked with reinvestigating the case. This began with officers pulling me from my cell one day to take a skin swab. The state wanted to see whether their dog-sniffing team could link my scent to the clothes taken from the victims after the crime. Those clothes had been kept in old paint cans, a method Burleson County used to store its evidence. The outcome of this investigation is easy to guess. The state claimed that even after nearly twenty years, the dogs had found my scent on the victims' clothing. It all felt too familiar. Batchelor and Kutnick seemed intent to follow Sebesta's lead in winning a conviction at all cost.

In the meantime, there'd been another shake-up in my representation. In September 2008, Jeff had withdrawn from my case for personal reasons. David had gone with him. Good to his word, though, Jeff had recruited Katherine Scardino and her partner Jimmy Phillips to replace him and David as my lead attorneys. Katherine came with a stellar record of vigorously defending her clients and had a reputation as a fighter who didn't back down from a challenge. Jimmy kind of flew under the radar, but he knew how to work the system, and he had a brilliant mind.

Nicole was still with me, loyal as ever, and my team gave me confidence. Katherine and Jimmy didn't share Nicole's sense of certainty in my innocence. They had to work up to that. Defense attorneys, I've learned, are trained to question everything, including their clients. Defendants lie at times, and old, savvy criminal defenders have heard it all. They went through my case file as most did. The layers of malfeasance revealed themselves in due course. A lying officer here, and a broken speaker there. In time, Katherine and Jimmy were certain, too, that they were representing an innocent man.

In 2009, a plea offer from the prosecutor arrived with a thud: if I pleaded guilty, they would commute my death sentence to life in prison. Batchelor didn't have much interest in trying the case to a verdict the second time around, but neither did he want to set me free. He did what I thought he might do: he offered me a life sentence as a way to end the case and avoid a new trial altogether.

"Anthony, I've got some news for you," Nicole told me during a visit to the jail. "Just know that as your attorney, I'm obligated to tell you all the offers. Here goes. The DA's offered you a life sentence."

"But what about giving me my freedom?" I asked.

"I knew you'd say no. I had to tell you anyway. Screw him and his life sentence. But there's something serious we have to think about. If the DA offers time served and your freedom in exchange for a guilty plea, would you be willing to take it?"

I thought about it for a while as I stared at the four walls around me. I'd been in one prison or jail or another for most of my adult life. My sons were then twenty-seven, twenty-eight, and thirty-two years old, and my oldest son Terrell had one son of his own. My youngest son Alex had three children. I'd missed being a father. I didn't want to miss being a grandfather too. During my incarceration, friends and family members had died. I was tired of listening to the Astros games behind prison walls. I was fed up with prison food. I missed female companionship. I would give anything in those moments to be able to throw my leg across my woman's leg at night.

"There are people out there that will always believe in your innocence," Nicole continued. "And some will always think you're guilty. I don't know how to advise you. I'll support you whatever decision you make."

I wanted my life back, but I didn't want the deal, were it to be offered me. Lies had put me behind bars and had kept me there. Lies had earned me the early life conviction that made it harder for me to get the opportunities I deserved. I had to live with myself. I'd rather die in that cage an honest man than walk out free a fraud.

"They're either going to kill me or set me free," I told Nicole. "There won't be a deal."

Her eyes widening, Nicole nodded as if she understood. We'd been on the same page since the first day she walked onto death row. Surely she didn't want to lose her friend, but she knew I'd rather die than lie to myself. Maybe I'd been desensitized to it all. There'd been so much death around me that I'd grown immune to it. I'd seen more than three hundred men go to their death. For years, they'd controlled me and the men on death row with fear. When I stopped fearing death, the jailers no longer had a hold on me. The decision was mine to stand on the firm foundation of the truth, rather than bending for the easy out.

Batchelor had an idea. He wanted me to take a lie-detector test, presumably to offload some of the guilt he felt over keeping me caged. If I passed the test, he said, they'd drop the charges. I'd seen this game before. A month later I found myself in the back of a cop car, heading to Dallas to test my truth. Nicole flew up to be with me for moral support. I was excited, of course. It felt like showing up for a math test knowing every question and all the answers. I knew they'd been playing games and that this could be another. I was willing to chance it, though, because it might just set me free.

The facility was different than what I was used to. It wasn't a jail. It was a commercial building, not far from town, with long hallways and snaking cubicles. They took me into a room, and I saw Nicole standing across the way. She gave me a nod and I smiled. The polygraph operator had been in law enforcement. He had quit to set up his own polygraph firm, and now he was assessing my results. This made me uneasy. My first polygraph had been examined by a man from the Texas Rangers. I knew how easy it was to interpret the test to get predetermined results. I had to stay calm. On death row, I'd developed little phrases, so-called life thoughts, to get me through the testier times. *God's got me*, I'd remind myself when I needed to stay calm. It settled me and centered me on the idea that I was protected from the storms around me.

The lead-up to the test was monotonous. The operator came in and out, asking me a handful of questions before retreating into some back room. I tried to imagine what he might be doing. I ate lunch right in the polygraph chair. I'd been up since around 3:30 a.m., and I spent many hours in that small room before the operator was finally ready to administer the test. He clamped the machine to my body and fired away with questions. For the first time in many years, I'd felt nervous. It was a strange phenomenon, fighting for my freedom again and again. I'd been fighting for many years, of course, but writing letters is very different than answering the questions of a state-administered polygraph. I answered fifteen minutes of questions before the operator left. My insides spun in knots. I'd felt nervous for several reasons. The main reason was that this could be the test that finally helped give me back my freedom. I couldn't sleep the night before. I was sure that I would pass the test and put myself in a position to regain my freedom. I was also nervous because the last time I offered to take a polygraph test they said that I had failed it, and I ended up on death row. I wasn't ready to trust Burleson County, but I had so little to lose.

Nicole entered not long after to tell me the somewhat unsurprising news, sadly: I'd failed the test.

Feelings of resentment and despair flooded in. It wasn't that particular test that brought me down but, rather, the cumulative effect of a thousand little setbacks. It felt like a carnival game rigged against me. Still, my expectations for the prosecutor's office were so low an ant could clear them. I knew that the fight would continue. There's some freedom in knowing the truth when others don't. I wanted to live, for sure, but if they killed me, I knew they'd have innocent blood on their hands.

I could tell that the test results had shaken Nicole. She lowered her head a bit, confused by the results. Deep down in the places where intimate knowledge of a crooked system hides, she knew that the state could make that test say whatever they needed it to say. On the surface, though, she was disappointed.

The prosecutor's approach had been transparent. He wanted to shake the faith my attorneys had in my innocence. Maybe if he could get my team to question whether I was truly innocent, they might back off and make the state's job easier. He didn't know Nicole, though, and he didn't know that she'd been fighting for my life for years. Even if she was shaken for an afternoon by the results of a single test, she had a half-decade of experience on the case to bring her back into the fold. My team wasn't deterred. Neither was I. I felt resolute in the commitment to fighting for my life.

The last-ditch attempt to manipulate my attorneys failed, and prosecutors dropped from the case like flies. The Attorney General's Office refused to pursue the case, giving the judge no official reason. Even Batchelor found a way out: citing health reasons, he removed himself, leaving the trial judge to find yet another special prosecutor. It was as if no one wanted to do the worst thing, but no one had the guts to do the right thing either.

JANUARY 2009–OCTOBER 2010:
FREEDOM WITHIN REACH

· · · · ·

JANUARY 2009 HAD BROUGHT a personnel change to the local DA's office. Bill Parham won the race in Burleson for district attorney, and though I didn't know him, I had reason to question the intentions of any person who would actually campaign to be the DA of that county. It was a matter of negative self-selection, I concluded. I didn't know where Parham stood on my case. In 2010, however, he and Judge Towslee-Corbett were able to select and hire a second special prosecutor. Kelly Siegler was brought in to handle the case.

Siegler was as hard-nosed a prosecutor as you'll find in Texas. She'd gained acclaim on the show *Cold Justice* and once won a death penalty trial by straddling a dummy and re-creating how in her view the defendant stabbed the victim. If there were fantasy leagues for death-seeking district attorneys, she'd be a top pick. With nineteen men sent to death row, Siegler had many scalps lining the wall of her office. I knew things had just gotten that much tougher for me.

New interest appeared around my case. During this time, journalist Pamela Colloff of the magazine *Texas Monthly* dug deep into my case file. She wanted to interview me for an upcoming story. When she visited, we talked for at least four hours about the dynamics of my case. I watched her mouth fall agape time after time as I recounted the ways that the prosecutor's office had procured my conviction. She tried to keep it neutral, to maintain her journalistic objectivity. After all, she wasn't writing a puff piece about a condemned man. She was writing in search of the truth. Beneath that journalistic facade, I could tell she believed in my innocence. We decided to stay in touch. She might need to ask follow-up questions for her story, and I sensed that she could be a powerful ally.

Weeks later, Pamela requested another visit to continue the interview. The sheriff denied her request. If I wanted her to return, I had to put her on my regular visitor list, which meant that our conversations would be monitored. The interview became impractical. We decided to correspond by mail instead. For a few months, we wrote back and forth. I answered her questions and offered some of my own. Pamela's faith in my story grew stronger, and she'd eventually use her pen to shine a light on what had happened.

Meanwhile, in July 2010, Kelly Siegler reached out to my team to request a meeting. No one knew why she wanted to meet, and Nicole was skeptical. Maybe she wanted to intimidate my lawyers. Perhaps she wanted to discuss a deal. As it turned out, the meeting was one giant game of poker. Neither side would reveal much. What we didn't know was that Siegler had come to believe in the possibility of my innocence. She set out, she claimed, to dot all the *i*'s and cross the *t*'s in hopes that she could secure a conviction that would stick. She walked away thinking she might have been handed the case of an innocent man. She'd called the meeting to help fill in some of the blanks in the story, though we didn't know it at the time.

Pamela Colloff's article "Innocence Lost" ran in *Texas Monthly* in October 2010. It penetrated the inner reaches of the Texas intelligentsia. Colloff meticulously examined the facts and contextualized all that had happened both inside and outside the courtroom. She wrote of the experience of hearing my words pour out in the weeks before my release. "As we talked, his story came tumbling out: about the Rangers, who were certain he was guilty, no matter what he said to the contrary; about the lineup, in which a woman he had never seen before had fingered him as the killer; about his trial, in which he listened to witnesses testify that he had confessed in jail to his guilt; about the souvenir knife, which the prosecution had held up as the murder weapon; about the man whose accusations against him could never be taken back, even after a dying declaration attesting to his innocence. We had been allotted two hours for our visit, but it was not enough."

Nicole drove all the way to Burleson County to deliver the article. The consequences of Pamela's writing were crucial to my fate. If she hit it out of the park, then people would notice, and public opinion would pressure the prosecutors to do the right thing for a change. I knew I didn't have many more chances. Pamela did hit a home run, though—and more. She told the public, for the first time, the true story of Anthony Graves, an innocent man railroaded nearly to death by a prosecutor intent on destructive injustice. This was a much-needed grand slam in my favor, it turned out.

It was finally my time. With public pressure mounting, Siegler did the unexpected. She called Nicole with her decision, as my legal team scrambled to get back to Burleson County.

On October 27, 2010, I learned the stunning news that the state had dropped all charges against me.

It was over. I was finally going home.

. . . . .

I would later learn more about how this decision came to be. Kelly Siegler had called in all her investigators one by one to see what they were thinking of my case. Each one she talked with told her that I was innocent. She met with District Attorney Parham, the newly elected Burleson DA who had hired her, to tell him that I was innocent.

I had been incarcerated since the week before my twenty-seventh birthday. I had lived behind prison walls for eighteen and a half years. I witnessed some of the worst inhumanity imaginable. I watched the state put men to death for crimes they might or might not have committed. I saw officers working behind those bars being treated hardly any differently than the inmates. I saw young boys grow into tired men. I observed families piling up in the visitation room to support a family member they knew would never come back home. I aged as our criminal justice system played politics with my life and the lives of hundreds of young men.

What I never witnessed during my eighteen and a half years in prison was justice. But finally, after surviving 6,640 days and two scheduled execution dates, and after witnessing hundreds of men executed around me, I was suddenly on my way home, without any preparation for a successful transition. I was scared out of my wits, but I was happy to be free.

As Nicole, Jimmy, and I drove out of the parking lot of the prison, Nicole's cell phone rang, and that alone took some time to get used to. Such a thing as a cell phone didn't exist when I went inside nearly two decades before, and now the person in the car with me driving me home from death row was able to receive a phone call as we pulled away, right there in her hand! On the phone was my old attorney Jeff Blackburn. He wanted to know if I would let him represent me in a civil lawsuit based on the wrongful conviction finding, which was basically an effort to get some money for all the horrible wrongs that the state had done to me.

I thought about it for a moment and decided that if anyone could get me some measure of financial compensation to stand in for real justice, it would be Jeff. He was a smart and aggressive attorney, and I knew that I would benefit from having him on my team in this capacity.

I told Nicole to tell him yes. But another legal proceeding was the last thing I wanted to be thinking about in that moment. Jimmy continued driving while I just looked out the window at a world that had changed on me. The houses seemed to be placed closer than I remembered, as though the world had grown and become crowded during those years. Cars looked different. Jimmy's car even talked to him! I could not have imagined that the last time I went for a ride, all those years ago.

It took us twenty minutes to reach my mom's house. As we pulled up, I noticed my cousins were standing in the front yard. They spotted me in the front seat and, in all their anticipation, made a mad dash to the car. I opened the door to big, warm, encompassing hugs, shrieks of joy, and lots of laughter. It was the raw kind of emotion that you could only experience; you couldn't really prepare for it, and it's difficult to describe it now in words. But you can imagine a bit of it, the most joyous basic expression of pure relief, happiness, and letting go that I had ever encountered, or probably ever will.

It felt good, but also strange. I hadn't been hugged by others like this, even family, in so long. I was looking around for my mom, but I didn't see her. Everyone was trying to catch my attention, handing me their cell phones in an effort to get me to speak to an old friend or acquaintance. I did my best to cope with it all, but it was overwhelming and hard to manage both inside and out.

My eldest son appeared. I had seen him grow up from behind bars, but it didn't really hit me how much I had lost until I was there hugging this grown man, who was also my own little boy. We embraced and I just held him, and the moment, as closely as I could.

All of a sudden, I heard someone say that my mother was there. She had left the house to tell my brother that I was on my way home, and now that she was back and excited to see me, she jumped out of the truck without putting it in gear to run over and give me a huge hug. Someone had to tell her that the car was rolling.

I can't begin to explain what it felt like to hug my mother after all those years. The state had put me and my entire family on death row, and now I was finally able to hug my mom and tell her that we were finally free of it; we were free. It was not easy to process more than eighteen years of a nightmare in those few moments of coming home. I knew I was OK now; I knew the feeling of relief. I began to try to let down my guard, but nearly two decades of living in intense survival mode left me unprepared for the transition. I was a bit lost, and while I coped with it, this was not really a celebration as much as me trying to deal with the massive overload of this grand moment.

An hour later, the entire yard was filled with people from the neighborhood. Friends that I had grown up with, family members, and others who just wanted to be a part of this feel-good moment. Nicole and Jimmy, and also Rick Ojeda, the investigator from my case who had worked so closely with the entire legal team, were becoming concerned about the crowd of people and the effect it might have been having on me, kind of like when a starved person is suddenly presented with too much food. It could be hard to take, even though it was a good thing that was happening.

They all wanted me to go somewhere that was a little quieter, to help get my feet under myself and to pace this experience out a little bit. I asked my family to come inside so that I could tell them I was calling it a night and leaving with Rick, who had offered to take me to his house. Of course, I would be back the next day to continue this reunion.

We all hugged good-bye, and then Rick and I drove down Highway 290 toward his home in Williamson County. I felt good, and I knew it was the right call to separate from the group for a bit on this first night. I was smiling as we drove down the highway. I was finally home, in the larger sense anyway. I didn't really know exactly where "home" was anymore, but I knew I was OK now, and in that sense, I had arrived.

Rick interrupted my thoughts and said that he was pulling into this convenience store to purchase something right quick. I watched as Rick got out of the truck and went into the store. Several people had walked in and out of the store before Rick came back out. He opened the door of the truck and handed me a bag. "You remember when I told you the first thing

I wanted to do when you got out?" Rick asked me. He'd said he wanted to be the first one to buy me a beer and to say, Welcome home, my friend. I looked into the bag to see a cold six-pack inside.

I could tell that Rick was a little emotional but quickly got himself back together. I told him that I would wait until we got to his home before I opened up a bottle of beer. Forty-five minutes later, we parked in front of Rick's house. When we walked in I could tell that someone was cooking inside. It was Rick's wife, Anya. She was preparing a meal of a roast and potatoes for us. Rick and I walked outside and sat on his patio. I could not believe I was sitting out under the night stars as a free man. Rick came out with two beers. We toasted and celebrated my release. We stayed up for several hours until it was time to go to bed.

There was going to be a big press conference in Houston the next day, and we had to get up early to make the three-hour drive to the big city. Rick showed me to a bedroom where I would be sleeping. It was a big queen-size bed with soft pillows and fresh sheets on it, something so common and so foreign to me at the same time, it was a little surreal. There was actual furniture in the room that I could sit on or lay on, and that was strange too, even though it wouldn't be to just about anyone else.

While it may have seemed the thing to do to stay at my mom's that first night out, for me, I just needed somewhere that I could go, a place that was away from all the stimulation. I had been on my own or with cellmates on death row for so long, that it was just overwhelming for me to suddenly enter a new world, as commonplace as it was for most other people. I needed a tiny bit of transition, and Rick's offer to stay with him provided that. It allowed me to catch my breath and my thoughts, while I tried to process the whirlwind that was happening to me.

Rick had left a fully charged cell phone with me to use for the night. I could make any call I wanted without asking, something of a novelty to a man in my position. He gave me a tour of the entire house including the bathroom where I could take a shower alone, for the first time in so very long. I was smiling from ear to ear the whole time because this was so far removed from the life that I had been living for two decades.

I finally got into bed to get some rest for the next day. I found it very hard to sleep. The bed was too soft and everything was too normal for me to doze off. I ended up calling my brothers and sisters on that cell phone laughing and talking for I don't know how long. I knew that they were all sleepy, but they were willing to stay up all night for me.

Finally, at about five in the morning, my body started to feel tired. I felt myself drifting off to sleep, but before closing my eyes, I thanked God for giving my life back to me.

ON JANUARY 20, 2014, Martin Luther King Jr. Day, three years after my exoneration, I held a press conference to announce that I would be filing a grievance against Charles Sebesta, the Texas prosecutor whose gross prosecutorial misconduct had led to my wrongful conviction. I'd been unable to file such a claim when I first got out of prison because of the statute of limitations. The time to file was seven years from the day of conviction, and I had spent eighteen and a half years in prison before the misconduct was ruled upon by the state.

However, thanks to Texas state senator Rodney Ellis and state representative Senfronia Thompson, the state passed a new law that would allow a grievance to be filed against a prosecutor within four years of a wrongfully imprisoned person's release. This was a much-needed reform indeed. I became the first exoneree to use this law in the State of Texas.

In May 2015, there was a hearing set for the misconduct grievance that I had filed with the Texas state Bar Association. They found probable cause to move forward. I hadn't seen Charles Sebesta in person since my late twenties, when he railroaded me out of my freedom. Now I was a forty-nine-year-old man.

Lydia Clay Jackson, one of my original trial attorneys, had been summoned to testify at this hearing. She and I were out in the hallway talking when Sebesta walked up to her. He had aged. He was no longer the man that I was angry at for stealing my life. He was an old man who walked halfway bent over. How could I want to punish this elderly man? I started feeling that this might not be the right thing to do. It appeared that this case had beaten him down. There had been numerous articles and documentaries throughout the years on my case, and they did not show Sebesta in the best light. After all, he did try to have an innocent man executed.

When Sebesta walked up to speak with Lydia, I interrupted to address him for the first time.

"Mr. Sebesta," I said. "I just want to say, no hard feelings," as I stuck my hand out for him to shake it. He looked at me as if I had surprised him, and he responded with a handshake so strong that I felt in my heart that it was the only apology he could offer. In that moment, Charles Sebesta had given me closure.

Thirty days later, in June 2015, the State of Texas disbarred Sebesta, prohibiting him from practicing law in Texas ever again.

I was finally free to move on.

My experience as a wrongfully convicted man has given me a perspective and insight few people will ever have about our criminal justice system and its need for reform. I met men like Nanon Williams, Anthony Pierce, Tony Ford, Arthur Brown, Rodney Reed, Howard Guidry, and others that I felt had compelling cases of innocence, but they remain in custody fighting for their lives, just as I had to do. I knew after my long stint on death row that I would go out into the free world and tell my story, with my face attached to it, to let people know why we need criminal justice reform.

I met men who were mentally disabled, kids who'd never even had sex yet on death row at seventeen. I left death row very concerned about the whole application of the death penalty. I didn't want to come out and challenge people's beliefs on the issue. I think they are entitled to feel about it whatever they want to and shouldn't be judged because of their position. The question I have is, Does the death penalty *work*?

I started the Anthony Graves Foundation to help inmates who have been wrongfully convicted or over-sentenced. My goal is to help find them lawyers who are willing to come on board and represent them pro bono. I get letters from inmates across our nation, and we can never have enough lawyers willing to take on this great work. My foundation also focuses on reentry work for men and women coming back home from prison. We partner with other organizations to outsource resources available in the area to those inmates reaching out to us who are trying to restart their lives.

I travel the globe sharing my story in front of thousands of people, organizations and businesses in hopes of bringing more awareness to the grave problems within our criminal justice system. It is my wish that *Infinite Hope* will inspire and encourage others always to know that this too shall pass and better days are always ahead for all of us.

MAY 2015

I sat in a Washington, DC, hotel room preparing for something I could never have imagined twenty years prior. I'd been asked by the ACLU to testify in front of Congress about the dangers of death row and the shadows of solitary confinement. When I took my seat in front of the microphone the next day, I worried about my back. The years of sleeping on metal cots had left permanent pains.

I spoke about finding glass in my food, and about the unthinkable madness that gripped some of the men who stayed too long. I stopped occasionally to collect myself. The memories of death row never left, but speaking about them gave the visions more heft. "Thank you for doing this," Illinois senator Dick Durbin said. "Together we're going to do something about this." It had been Senator Durbin who called the congressional hearing in the first place, to examine the use of solitary confinement. When he asked me to testify about my experience in solitary, and how I dealt with it, I agreed to come in and give my testimony, and now here was a United States senator thanking *me* for talking about those painful days.

That moment wasn't the start of my mission, but it steeled my desire to use my freedom for something bigger. Things have changed a lot since I walked out of jail in October 2010. The state paid out a sum of money designed to compensate me for the lost years. I've used that money to launch the Anthony Graves Foundation, where I continue my work to this day.

Together with a community of supporters, we worked to free Alfred Dwayne Brown, who'd been sentenced to death for a murder he didn't commit. In my travels and speaking engagements, I'm often asked what kept me alive on death row. Through faith, I found purpose and preparation. I couldn't control much about the process. The lies told on the stand might have sent me away, but they couldn't follow my mind into the interior of my cell. True faith inspires purpose and leads to preparation.

As I watched men go out of their minds on death row, and as I learned their stories, I saw broken little boys who'd once dreamed of stealing second base. I learned to view them in terms of their pain, knowing that, for the vast majority, all the pain they'd caused to victims could be traced to childhood trauma and a history of abuse, as well as a lack of any real opportunity or support. I came to see my fellow inmates as the abandoned few, left behind by their schools, families, and communities. Surely some were innocent, but even the men who weren't had at some point been redeemable.

My faith told me that I'd be getting out eventually, and even if I didn't, my story could inspire people to care about a system that lays waste to the lives of victims and defendants alike. My purpose was clear. I'd fight to tell the stories of the innocents left behind, and of the young boys abandoned before they ever reached death row. I would fight to reform a criminal justice system that had turned criminal against its own citizens. I would use my voice to bring attention to the inhumane treatment behind prison bars where men are treated as though they no longer have rights in this country. I would bring attention to the mental illness issues that run rampant behind those walls. My purpose became promoting fairness and effecting reform throughout the criminal justice system. I would use my story to help enlighten the rest of the world.

In my faith in God, I found preparation. I remember receiving my first execution date at Ellis Unit. I had been lying on my bunk reading Paulo Coelho's *Veronika Decides to Die*, when two officers approached my cell door. They'd been instructed to bring me to the major's office. I stood up, stripped naked, and went through the dehumanizing process of a strip search. I was asked to hand them my boxers, socks, shoes, and white jumpsuit with the black letters on the back that said DEATH ROW. After going through the search, I was handed back my clothes and asked to get dressed. I raised my boxers up just high enough so that when I shook them out the wind would blow toward the officer's nose. It was one of our ways of protesting the strip search. I put my clothes on. I was then asked to turn around and put my hands through the bean slot in the center of the door. I was then handcuffed, stood up straight, turned around to face the officers as they called out to the picket officer to roll my door ("Roll one, row 15 cell!"). The picket officer hit the button and my door rolled open. I walked out with my wrists handcuffed behind my back, and two officers with batons escorted me to the major's office. The major entered, took a seat across the desk from me, and informed me that the State of Texas had set an execution date.

The state could set multiple execution dates for me, but no jailer could stop me from refining a message of faith and perseverance to be used on the outside. I practiced night after night, planning what I might say to young men and women who strayed off the straight and narrow. I didn't know when I'd get an opportunity to speak as a free man, but I continued to prepare for when that time came. If death row had taught me anything, it was the value of time. Attorneys often came right down to the wire seeking stays for their clients. Minutes and hours meant life and death. I knew then there was no time to lose. Preparedness doesn't depend on circumstances. Even the condemned man with an actual death sentence can prepare for the future. It was through faith that I knew my practice was not a wasted effort.

I sustained myself through the longest nights with the simple assurance that God is good. And now that I'm living as a free man, I know this to be true. I've been blessed with opportunities to travel the world and tell my story. I've been asked to speak in front of national and international audiences. I'm doing the work I was meant to do—sharing my story in hopes that all of you out there will keep the faith, find your purpose, and prepare for the opportunity to effect change in a world that desperately needs reform.

．　．　．　．　．

I've been truly blessed since coming home. One of my proudest achievements is launching the Anthony Graves Foundation, which is geared toward making positive change throughout the criminal justice system. My foundation, located in Houston, Texas, has three main programs. First, the Humane Investigation Project, or HIP, is a program I established to help those who have been wrongfully convicted by finding pro bono attorneys willing to take their cases. One of the greatest obstacles for people in my position on death row is that you feel you can't get help because you don't have money. Too often, that's true. HIP is aimed at helping connect qualified attorneys to truly needy inmates, without the burden of money. There are generous lawyers who donate this vital service, and I help locate them.

Second, my foundation has a Re-entry Program established to arrange counseling and wraparound services for women and girls returning from incarceration. It was a choice I made based on the fact that women are forgotten in our criminal justice system. The plan is to expand it to address the needs of men and boys as well.

Finally, my foundation has an Exoneree Speakers Bureau, where we teach exonerees how to tell their stories to have the most impact. It's a small part in our efforts to reform a broken system, yet this program is particularly rewarding. I can see huge progress in the exonerees' self-confidence, communication skills, and overall improvement of self-image. For men whose shoes I have stood in myself, it is deeply satisfying to witness the transformation.

I've been able to have an impact on people's lives all over the world through sharing my story. After my release, I took a job with the Texas Defender Service as an investigator. From there, I was able to help get the next innocent man after me off Texas death row! Alfred Brown's key alibi witness shared information with me that I then provided to his attorneys, and this led to Brown's release. I also became a public speaker in high demand. I started speaking at conferences for law enforcement, DA's offices, defense attorney associations, and big law firms. I've traveled to places as far away as Italy, Switzerland, Sweden, Germany, and France to tell my story. I've spoken in some of the largest and oldest churches. I've spoken at prestigious universities, such as Yale, Emory, the University of Texas, the University of Bern (Switzerland), Cornell, and Texas Tech. I once introduced Supreme Court justice Stephen Breyer at an awards ceremony in Washington, DC, hosted by the American Bar Association (ABA). I wrote an article for *Time* magazine.

I've spoken before the Senate Judiciary Committee at the request of Senators Dick Durbin, Al Franken, and Lindsey Graham about the effects of solitary confinement. I've sat on panels hosted by the ABA and the American Civil Liberties Union focused on criminal justice reform. I've been a keynote speaker for events hosted by organizations such as the Anti-Defamation League, Amnesty International, the Texas Coalition to Abolish the Death Penalty, the American Academy of Psychiatry and Law, and the Houston Forensic Science Center. And I've done more television appearances than I can count, both in the United States and abroad. My story was featured on *48 Hours* in an episode titled "Grave Injustice," which won an Emmy Award.

I am proud to have created a scholarship fund in honor of the lady who saved my life. The Nicole B. Cásarez Scholarship Fund at the University of Texas will help train young people who aspire to become criminal defense attorneys. Nicole is the model they should all aspire to—her heart and her mind are in exactly the right place for this weary world.

. . . . .

I spent a lot of time reading books during my incarceration. In general, books that gave me fresh insight into life are the ones I admired most, but I read a lot of law books too. These are the titles that stand out:

- *The Alchemist* by Paulo Coelho: This book reminded me of the journey I wanted to travel when I came home. It reminded me that everything I needed in this world was already within me.
- *Veronika Decides to Die* by Paulo Coelho: It reminded me that you must be careful what you ask for in life because you just might get it.
- *The Pilgrimage* by Paulo Coelho: Like so many of his writings, this book gave me a spiritual connection to something higher than myself.
- *The Autobiography of Martin Luther King Jr.*: Taught me about inner strength.
- *The Autobiography of Malcolm X* (as told to Alex Haley): Taught me about fighting back against a system out to kill me.
- *The Mis-Education of the Negro* by Carter G. Woodson: Opened my eyes to the importance of investing back into our communities.
- *Incidents in the Life of a Slave Girl* by Harriet Jacobs: One of my all-time favorite books! Jacobs was a slave, and she wrote about escaping to freedom. I gained a lot of strength from her described struggles.
- *The Measure of a Man* by Sidney Poitier: Reinforced the value of my family.
- *Soul on Ice* by Eldridge Cleaver: Taught me a lot about race relationships from the perspective of a black man.
- *Dreams from My Father* by Barack Obama: Made me feel hopeful about good things happening from bad situations; it was like giving me fuel when I needed some most.
- *The Audacity of Hope* by Barack Obama: Made me feel proud to read a book by our first black president.
- *Native Son* by Richard Wright: Gave me insight into racism before the civil rights era.
- *Love and Lies* by Kimberla Lawson Roby: Made me sit, cross my legs, and read about God and relationships.
- *The Ways of White Folks* by Langston Hughes: Painful and funny about racism and white people.
- *Loving* by Henry Green: Good novel that talked about things outside the US, which allowed me to travel abroad in my mind.

- *Go Tell It on the Mountain* by James Baldwin: Drew emotions out of me that spoke volumes to my own black experience.
- *The 48 Laws of Power* by Robert Greene: I read this book and felt that I already knew everything it was talking about; it made me feel right.
- *Maximize the Moment* by T. D. Jakes: I read his books when I needed to feel inspired on a spiritual level.
- The Bible: For peace and a sense of purpose.
- *Thieves' Paradise* by Eric Jerome Dickey: For when I felt like watching television and didn't have one.
- *Roots* by Alex Haley: I loved reading this book for the first time. It was better than the TV series I had watched many years before.
- *For the Love of Money* by Omar Tyree: Relaxed me and made me feel like I was watching a movie.
- *The Celestine Prophecy* by James Redfield: A thoughtful and provocative book, particularly given the isolation of my environment while reading it.

ACKNOWLEDGMENTS

THERE ARE SO MANY PEOPLE that I would like to thank for making my freedom possible.

First, there's no possible way I could have done this without God being my shining light throughout the darkest corners of my life. I also must thank my mom for being the best mother that she could be under those circumstances. You kept my spirits up and encouraged me along the way to never give up. I love and deeply appreciate you always for that.

Thank you Isabelle Perin for coming into my life and showing me the true meaning of unconditional love. You will always shine brightly in my world.

Thank you Nicole Cásarez for being the greatest attorney who ever walked into my life! And then for becoming my big sister and my angel along the way. You should run for governor of Texas. I am forever grateful.

Thank you Neal Manne from the Susman Godfrey law firm for taking up my cause and seeking justice. It is because of you, Charles Eskridge at Quinn Emanuel law firm, and Kathryn Kase that Charles Sebesta is now disbarred and can never harm another innocent man again. I owe you my deep gratitude.

Thank you Kelly Siegler for having the guts to stand up and do the right thing for justice. My family and I thank you deeply for giving us back our freedom.

Thank you Pamela Colloff for writing an amazing article on my story that revealed the truth about my wrongful conviction. In my estimation, you are the best journalist on the planet.

Thank you Coby DuBose for helping prepare my story for book form.

Thank you to my manager, David Kuhn; literary agent, David McCormick; and editor, Rakia Clark, and everyone at Beacon Press for helping me get this book across the finish line. I appreciate all your efforts.

Thank you Marina Vorlander, Lars Augustsson, Nick Bell, Katherine Scardino, and Jimmy Phillips Jr.

Most importantly, I thank my sons for always believing in me from the first day. I love you guys deeply.

I couldn't end this without sending a shout-out to all the men and women who are behind bars fighting for justice. Keep your heads up, and keep your spirits up, because your freedom is possible.